Fast & Fun
Scrap Crafts™

Edited by Laura Scott

HOUSE of
WHITE
BIRCHES

PUBLISHERS
SINCE 1947

Fast & Fun Scrap Crafts

Editor: Laura Scott
Contributing Editor: Maria Nerius
Associate Editor: Cathy Reef
Design Manager: Vicki Blizzard
Technical Editor: Läna Schurb
Copy Editors: Michelle Beck, Nicki Lehman, Mary Martin
Publication Coordinators: June Sprunger, Tanya Turner

Photography: Tammy Cromer-Campbell
Photography Assistant: Linda Quinlan

Graphic Arts Supervisor: Ronda Bechinski
Book/Cover Design: Jessi Butler
Graphic Artist: Edith Teegarden
Production Assistants: Janet Bowers, Marj Morgan
Traffic Coordinator: Sandra Beres
Technical Artists: Liz Morgan, Mitch Moss, Travis Spangler, Chad Summers

Publishers: Carl H. Muselman, Arthur K. Muselman
Chief Executive Officer: John Robinson
Publishing Marketing Director: David McKee
Book Marketing Manager: Craig Scott
Product Development Director: Vivian Rothe
Publishing Services Director: Brenda R. Wendling
Publishing Services Manager: Brenda Gallmeyer

Printed in the United States of America
First Printing: 2002
Library of Congress Number: 2001097993
ISBN: 1-882138-92-9

A Note From the Editor

All of us crafters have something in the closet—oodles and oodles of leftover craft supplies! It seems that any project we make doesn't quite use up all the supplies we purchased to make it. My craft closet (OK, i'll be honest—it is a craft room the size of about six closets!) is filled with wood, paints, watercolor pencils, foam, felt, fabric, pom-poms, glue, glitter and … well, you get the idea.

What better idea for a book than one with projects specially designed from and for using up all those scrap odds and ends? Not only will you save money with these projects, but also you'll free up lots of space for new supplies!

So here you have it—a collection of the best and brightest designs from our top designers, plus handy hints and tips from one of today's leading craft experts, Maria Nerius. The projects included reflect today's trends: upscale but not uptight; up-to-date but not trendy; warm and friendly but not silly.

You'll find many ideas for dressing up your home's interiors. Give your favorite room a decorator look without the decorator's price! Enjoy creating one-of-a-kind gifts for sharing with your family and loved ones. Not only will they appreciate your thoughtfulness, but you may pick up a new crafting buddy or two along the way!

And for your holiday celebrations, discover the joy of making each special occasion extra fun and festive!

Whether you use the projects in this book as actual patterns to follow, or simply to get ideas for launching your own creative spirit, we hope you enjoy this collection of quick and easy-to-make scrap crafts!

Warm regards,

Laura Scott

Contents

Chapter 1
Spring Fling!

Chapter 2
Summer Sparkles!

Spring Fling!

Add zest and life to spring with this collection of fun-to-craft scrap projects! Cheerful holiday designs, breezy home accents, quick-to-make bazaar projects and much more will turn your crafting scraps into delightful treasures!

The Joys of Scrap Crafting

Is it possible that you might be able to use that scrap for a future project?

By Maria Nerius

In the art world, a "found object" is anything you might "find" and then add to an art piece. Usually, found objects are seen in collages or mixed media work. They add interest, texture and dimension to craft projects, too.

I enjoy collage work, and I've come to the conclusion that a "found object" is often nothing more than a scrap of something left over from one of my other projects.

Most of us are scrap crafters at heart; I know I am! I have a small tackle box that is filled with miscellaneous beads. I've got a bag of fancy threads and simple floss snippets. My craft table has a drawer jammed full of remnants of handmade, acid-free and embossed papers in every color of the rainbow. I have glass jars full of assorted buttons, jewelry findings and wooden cutouts. I save all my floral leftovers, including buds and leaves.

In short, *nothing* leaves my craft area if it is possibly usable. You never know when a scrap might come in handy—and we crafters pride ourselves in *always* being ready!

Though not a formal rule, most crafters get a kick out of making something creative from what appears to the average person as junk headed for the trash can. In fact, scrap crafting is a delightful form of recycling; if thrown away, those scraps would end up in a landfill.

So, scrap crafting works hand in hand with the crafter's creed: "Recycle and waste not." There's real joy to be found in creating something from scraps of paper, fabric, wood, plastic, clay, glass and other crafting supplies.

Before you get ready to toss those bits of felt, lob that almost empty bottle of paint, or pitch that button that has no match, ask yourself a simple question: "Is it possible that I might be able to use this item for a future project?" You just need to learn to look at all your precious "found" items in a creative light. And don't worry if you can't figure out what to do with all those scraps you've been hoarding and storing for that rainy-day craft project, because we're going to give you lots of tips and ideas to help you do just that! ✄

The Master Scrap List

You probably don't need a list, but we're hoping you might get a few ideas from ours. In scrap crafting, your only limit is your imagination—yet sometimes a good list comes in handy. All you need is a fragment, a wisp, a morsel, a slice, a piece or a part to get your imagination running!

- Batting
- Beads
- Buttons
- Candle stubs
- Chenille stems
- Craft foam
- Craft wire
- Crayons
- Essential or fragrance oils
- Fabric

- Felt
- Jewelry findings
- Lace
- Leather
- Markers
- Ribbon
- Shells
- Snaps and other fasteners
- Soap slivers
- Spices

- Spools
- Threads and flosses
- Trims
- Paint
- Paper
- Pinecones
- Plastic, dried or silk flowers
- Pompoms
- Wood turnings and cutouts
- Yarn

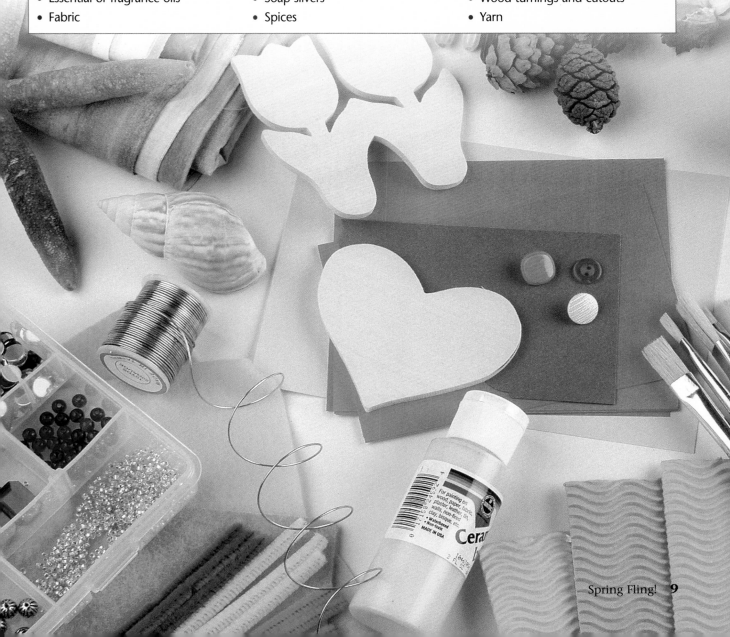

Mini Keepsake Journals

Scraps of decorative papers and other odds and ends make sweet booklets for saving special snapshots, messages from friends, or other memorabilia.

Designs by Marilyn Gossett

Materials

Each Journal

- 2 (4") squares poster board
- Card stock: ivory, white
- 4 (8½" x 4") rectangles résumé paper or stationery
- Glue stick
- Tacky glue
- Ultrafine-point black permanent marker
- Stylus or round toothpick
- 1 yard coordinating ¼"-wide ribbon

Remember Me

- 3½" square poster board
- Memory book papers*: lavender-on-lavender stripe, yellow gingham and blue-on-blue polka dots
- Small scalloped paper edgers
- Wooden cutouts*: 1¼" circle, 2 (¾") circles, 1⅛" heart
- Acrylic paints*: Santa's flesh, white, black, bright red, mello yellow, lilac, light foliage green, nectar coral, pigskin
- Acrylic varnish*
- Paintbrushes: #8 shader, #1 round
- Small lavender paper flower

Our Family

- Memory book papers*: pink-and-yellow gingham and blue-on-blue polka dots
- Card stock: 5" square ivory, 6" square white
- Scalloped paper edgers
- Acrylic paint*: blue heaven
- Small pink paper flower

Paper Pizzazz paper by Hot Off the Press; Woodsies cutouts from Forster; Ceramcoat paints from Delta.

Remember Me Journal

1. *Covers:* From striped paper, cut two 5" squares. Center one 4" square of poster board on wrong side of one piece of paper. Miter corners and fold paper over edges of poster board; glue. Repeat to make second cover.

2. Glue front cover right side up in center of ivory card stock. Trim card stock with scalloped edgers, leaving ¼" border.

3. *Binding:* Cut 4" x 3" striped paper. Fold lengthwise into thirds, folding sides toward middle; glue.

4. Lay covers right side down and side by side, leaving ¼" gap between edges. Apply glue to inner edges of covers; lay binding strip over open seam, adhering to both covers. Smooth firmly; let glue dry.

5. Close journal, pressing binding so journal lays flat.

6. *Inner covers:* Cut 4" x 8" striped paper with stripes perpendicular to long edges. Glue inside journal covers to cover raw edges; smooth in place.

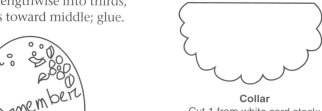

Sign
Cut 1 from white card stock

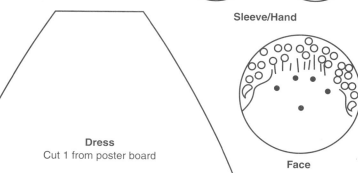

Dress
Cut 1 from poster board

Collar
Cut 1 from white card stock;
trim curve with scalloped paper edgers

Sleeve/Hand

Face

Shoes

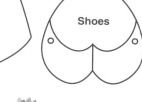

7. *Pages:* Fold résumé paper in half; insert between covers. Hold pages in place by wrapping ribbon around fold, and binding and tying ends in a simple bow near top of journal, leaving 1" tails; trim tails at an angle.

Doll

1. *Painting:* Referring to patterns throughout, paint larger circle (face) flesh; paint half of each small circle yellow (sleeves) and other half flesh (hands). Paint heart black along curves for shoes and flesh elsewhere.

2. *Face and shoes:* Blush cheeks with coral (see "Painting Techniques" in the General Instructions, page 174). Using stylus dipped in paint, dot on black eyes and red mouth; highlight eyes and cheeks with tiny white dots. Paint hair pigskin. Dot white buttons onto shoes. Apply varnish to shoes; let dry.

3. *Flowers in hair:* Dot on clusters of four lavender dots for each flower; dot middle of each with white. Add

tiny green leaves with #1 brush.

4. *Sleeve trim:* Dot white paint down yellow side of center line on each sleeve.

5. *Sign:* Cut sign from white card

stock. Glue wrong side to right side of a larger piece of blue polka-dot paper; trim with scalloped edgers to make sign frame. Paint flowers, leaves and hearts on sign as shown.

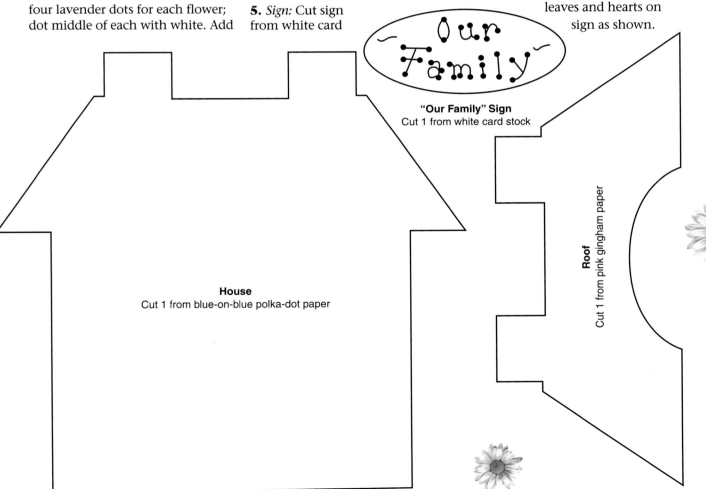

"Our Family" Sign
Cut 1 from white card stock

House
Cut 1 from blue-on-blue polka-dot paper

Roof
Cut 1 from pink gingham paper

6. Using black marker, add "Remember Me" lettering; outline sign with dot-dash line. Also outline sleeves with scalloped trim, hands, face, and flowers and leaves in hair. Define feet with line drawn up center of heart.

7. *Dress:* Cut dress from poster board; cover with yellow gingham paper as in step 1 of journal instructions, folding edges of paper to back and gluing. (Clip paper as needed around curves so edges are smooth.)

8. *Lace trim:* Glue hem of dress to white card stock; use scalloped edgers to trim off all but a ¼" border around hem for lace trim. Using scalloped edgers, cut collar from white card stock. Dot lavender paint onto each curve of scalloped edges; let dry.

Assembly

Glue feet, dress, collar, head, arms and sign to journal's front cover as shown. Glue lavender flower to collar off to one side.

Our Family Journal

1. Repeat step 1 as for Remember Me journal, substituting lavender-on-lavender stripe for blue-on-blue polka dot.

2. *Roof:* Referring to patterns throughout, cut roof from gingham paper. Glue wrong side to right side of a larger piece of white card stock; trim all around with scalloped edgers to frame roof. Glue roof to front cover positioning edge of roof 1½" down from top of cover.

3. *Inner covers:* Cut two 3⅜" squares from gingham paper; glue one inside each cover to cover raw edges; smooth in place.

4. Cut one house from blue-on-blue polka-dot paper; matching edges, glue inside front cover.

5. Repeat steps 3–5 as for Remember Me journal, substituting lavender stripe paper for blue-on-blue polka-dot.

6. Repeat step 7 as for Remember Me journal.

7. *Sign:* Cut sign from white card stock. Glue wrong side to right side of a larger piece of ivory card stock; trim with scalloped edgers to make sign frame. Using stylus dipped in paint, dot blue paint onto each curve of scalloped edges; let dry.

8. Using black marker, add Our Family lettering to center of sign.

9. Glue sign to front of journal; glue pink flower above sign. ✂

Don't Throw Out That Paper!

Save time and money by conserving your paper crafting materials!

Paper used to be fairly inexpensive, but that's not always the case today—especially when you get into handmade and acid-free papers. Understandably, then, it just kills the typical crafter to throw away this staple of creativity. But there are so many ways to use up those scraps of paper—even the itty-bitty pieces!

• *Paper Mosaics:* Use patterns from traditional mosaics and even stained-glass patterns to re-create the design using paper. This is also called paper quilting.

• *Mats:* Scrapbookers use smaller pieces of acid-free papers as mats for photos and journaling on scrapbook pages. If you need a larger mat, piece one together for a quilted look.

• *Paper Dolls:* They're the rage again! Use paper scraps to make clothes and accessories for this old-time favorite.

• *Scratch Sheets:* My mom used to call scrap paper a scratch sheet. She used the paper to practice brush strokes, spacing lettering and sketching project ideas.

• *Gift Tags:* Who doesn't need gift tags? Get creative and make your own!

• *Beads:* Make paper beads by

wrapping squares, rectangles and triangles of paper around a toothpick.

• *Tea-bag Folding:* This is a great paper craft, and you can create one-of-a-kind projects with scraps!

• *Paper-Making:* Yes! You can recycle scraps of paper into your own handmade paper. All you need is a blender, water and a paper screen.

• *Confetti:* Use paper punches to punch a handful of confetti to add to a letter or greeting card. Don't have punches? Just cut small geometrical and random shapes with scissors.

• *Shredded Filler:* Shred sheets of used paper to use as filler in floral designs and gift baskets.

• *Weaving:* Weave together long strips for backgrounds in card-making and rubber-stamping. ✂

Victorian Tea Basket

Here's a great way to use some of those extra baskets and jars you've collected!

Design by Samantha McNesby

Materials

- 7" round wicker basket
- Shredded white tissue paper
- Tea bags
- Scone mix: 1½ cups white flour, 2¼ teaspoons baking powder, 3 tablespoons sugar, ½ cup raisins
- 1-pint glass jar with lid
- 6" circle pink fabric

- 18" white gathered lace
- Small amount fiberfill
- 1 yard ¼"-wide metallic gold wire-edged ribbon
- Rubber band
- Needle and thread
- 4" x 7" parchment or other paper
- Acrylic craft paints: ivory, light pink, light blue, metallic gold

- Miniature wooden teapot*
- Acrylic sealer
- 2 small rose and flower decals*
- 1" foam brush
- Small round paintbrush

Miniature teapot #3399 from Walnut Hollow; #1055 Cabbage Rose Handpainted Look decal from Plaid.

Continued on page 15

Beaded Candle Set

Inexpensive candles take on an elegant flair when you add beads and a simple, painted candle box.

Designs by Samantha McNesby

Materials

Box

- 5" x 7½" wooden candle box with heart-shaped cutout
- Acrylic craft paints*: glorious gold, white wash, pale pink
- 1-step crackle medium*
- 1" foam brush
- Small round or liner paintbrush
- 24" silver wire in 20-, 22- or 24-gauge
- 37 pale pink glass "E" beads
- 27 round plastic 8mm faceted "crystal" beads*
- Wire snips or old scissors

Candle

- 3" white pillar candle
- Approximately 140 1" flat-topped dressmaker's silk straight pins
- Pink pearl-finish "E" beads
- Clear glass 10/0 seed beads
- White glass 10/0 seed beads
- Thimble

Americana and Dazzling Metallics paints, and Weathered Wood crackle medium, all from DecoArt; plastic faceted beads from The Beadery.

Project Notes

If your box does not have holes for a handle, drill ⅟₁₆" hole in center of opposite sides of box ½" below top. Remove any existing handle with wire cutters before proceeding.

Follow manufacturer's instructions for using crackle medium; otherwise, let paints dry between applications.

Box

1. Paint box exterior gold with foam brush. Apply crackle medium; when dry, top with white paint. Paint will crackle as it dries.

2. Using foam brush, paint inside of box pink; paint pink stripes the width of foam brush around outside of box, leaving 1" white stripes between them.

3. Using liner, add gold squiggly lines and tiny hearts between stripes.

Handle

1. Thread three pink beads onto end of wire; feed one end of wire through one of the holes in box from outside to inside, leaving 6" tail. Add two more pink beads to wire tail; twist wire end around wire several times to hold handle in place.

2. Beginning with "crystal" bead, string wire alternately with crystal and pink beads until all crystal

beads are used, and ending with pink bead.

3. String two more pink beads onto wire; run wire through remaining hole from outside to inside; string three more pink beads onto wire tail and twist wire end to secure handle as in step 1.

4. Snip off wire tails.

Candle

1. Using pin as stylus and ruler or small T-square to keep lines straight, *lightly* scratch vertical guidelines down the surface of the candle about every ½" around the candle. (Sample candle has 17 rows.)

2. Thread one clear bead and then one pink bead onto a pin. Using thimble-covered finger, press pin

straight into candle along one of the guidelines. Repeat to press eight beaded pins evenly spaced down vertical guideline.

3. Repeat step 2 to fill the next vertical row in the same manner as the first.

4. Fill third row with eight beaded pins, each threaded with one clear bead, one white bead and one clear bead. Continue pattern of two pink rows and one white row around candle until filled. (Sample ends with a single pink row.)

5. Set candle inside box. Candle may be burned as usual, but do not carry box with burning candle inside, and do not leave burning candle unattended. ✂

Victorian Tea Basket

Continued from page 13

Scone Mix

1. Clean and dry jar and lid.

2. Combine all ingredients for scone mix; spoon or pour into jar, tapping jar to settle ingredients. Ingredients will completely fill jar. Seal jar securely with lid.

3. Sew lace to edge of fabric circle. Place fiberfill on top of jar lid; top with fabric circle and secure with rubber band.

4. Cut 24" piece gold ribbon; tie

around lid in a bow, concealing rubber band; do not trim ribbon tails.

5. Copy the following instructions onto parchment:

Scones

Scone mix

⅓ cup margarine or butter

1 egg, beaten

¼ cup half-and-half

Heat oven to 400 degrees.

Pour scone mix into medium-size bowl. Cut butter into scone mix using a pastry blender or fork, until mixture resembles fine crumbs. Stir in beaten egg and half-and-half, stirring just until dough leaves sides of bowl. Add a bit more half-and-half, if needed.

Turn the dough onto a lightly floured surface. Knead lightly about 5 times. Pat into a rectangle about ½" thick. Use a sharp knife to cut the dough into triangles. (A biscuit cutter may also be used.) Place on ungreased baking sheet.

Bake scones 10–12 minutes, until

golden brown. Remove from baking sheet and cool. Serve with butter and preserves.

6. Roll parchment into scroll and secure with gold ribbon tied in a bow; trim ribbon tails.

Teapot

1. Using foam brush, base-coat teapot with ivory (see "Painting Techniques" in the General Instructions, page 174); let dry. Paint lower part of teapot and lid edges light pink; paint handle, spout and knob light blue. Let dry

2. Using small brush, outline top, bottom, handle, spout and sides of lid with gold; let dry

3. Apply decal to front and back of teapot.

4. Coat teapot with sealer.

Assembly

Fill bottom of basket with shredded tissue paper. Arrange scone mix, teapot, scroll with instructions and some pretty teabags in basket. Coil long ribbon ends from scone jar around basket handles. ✂

Princess Sign

Please your resident royalty with this quick and easy plaque for the door or wall of her "royal bedchamber."

Design by Samantha McNesby

Materials

- 7" x 5" wooden plaque with scalloped edges
- Acrylic craft paints: white, pale pink, medium pink
- 1" foam brush
- ¼" flat brush
- Metallic gold paint pen or gold paint and fine round brush
- 12" gold chain
- 12 (¼") flat-back clear rhinestones or crystals
- 1 teardrop chandelier crystal with gold metal hook
- ¼" gold eye hook
- Thick white glue
- Heavy-duty stapler

Instructions

1. Using foam brush, paint sides and top of plaque light pink; let dry. Paint sides medium pink; let dry. Using flat brush, add white stripes around edges; let dry.

2. Referring to "Using Transfer and Graphite Paper" in the General Instructions, page 174, transfer lettering to front of sign; fill in with gold paint pen. Using paint pen, add thin line around beveled edge; let dry.

3. Glue rhinestones on top near scalloped edge.

4. *Hanger:* Staple ends of chain to back of sign, using several staples on each end.

5. Screw eye hook into center bottom of plaque. Attach crystal to eye hook, using crystal's existing hardware. ✂

Princess Sign

Vintage Button Box

Dress up a simple little box with odd buttons for a fetching trinket holder or gift package.

Design by Joan Fee

Materials
- Small, round, white, fabric-covered box with padded lid
- Gold spray webbing
- Tacky glue
- Assorted buttons

Instructions

1. Remove lid from box. Following manufacturer's instructions, spray box and lid with webbing. Let dry.

2. Glue buttons on lid in desired arrangement. Let dry. ✂

Light Up Your Spring!

Use your scraps to create dazzling candles!

Scraps from jewelry and other craft projects make great embellishments for store-bought candles.

Gather assorted beads, stones, charms, glitter and anything else that isn't highly flammable and mix it together on a small cookie sheet with sides. Apply jewelry or tacky glue to the bottom half of a candle, then roll the candle in the mixture. Lift several times to see if you are missing any glued areas. Allow to dry completely.

This can be a messy process, but the results are worth it! The candle can then be placed in a holder or centerpiece. The candlelight reflects beautifully off the beads and glitter. Just remember never to leave a candle unattended while it is burning.

To make the candles last longer, place them in the refrigerator for several hours before burning for a slower, cleaner burn!

Embossed Candle Rings

Soft aluminum is easy to "emboss" with the aid of a stylus and stencils.
Leave as is or touch with color to accent any candle beautifully.

Designs by Paula Bales

Materials

Each Candle

- 36-gauge .005 soft aluminum*
- Stylus
- Craft cement

Color-Kissed Roses

- Rose stencil*
- Craft paints*: bubble gum, kelly green
- #10 shader paintbrush
- Push pin
- Soft cloth
- 6" pink pillar candle
- 30" fine silver craft cord

Dragonflies & Bees

- Dragonflies and bees stencil*
- 2¼" light green pillar candle

Soft aluminum from K&S Engineering; Apple Barrel craft paints and Simply Laser Stencils from Plaid.

Color-Kissed Roses Candle Ring

1. Cut aluminum strip 1¾" x 10½" (or correct size to fit your candle).

2. Repositioning stencil as necessary, use stylus to emboss roses down center of aluminum strip; add top and bottom borders.

3. Emboss a larger single rose on another small piece of aluminum; cut out and poke hole in top with push pin.

4. Paint roses pink and leaves green; let dry. Gently rub off paint with soft cloth, leaving color in recessed areas.

5. Wrap aluminum band around bottom of candle; glue overlapped ends together.

6. String silver cord through hole in single rose; wrap cord around candle and tie in a bow.

Dragonflies & Bees Ring

1. Cut aluminum strip 1¼" x 9½" (or correct size to fit your candle).

2. Repositioning stencil as necessary, use stylus to emboss dragonflies and bees down center of aluminum strip; add top and bottom borders.

3. Wrap aluminum band around bottom of candle; glue overlapped ends together. ✂

Sparkling Candle Collars

Beautiful foils in jewel colors make it easy to create dazzling ornaments
that add beauty to your table as they glitter in the candlelight.

Designs by Debba Haupert

Materials

- 9" x 6" foil*: mint, violet
- 26-gauge tinned copper (silver) wire*
- Stylus or other pointed tool
- Craft knife
- Knitting needle or similar round object
- Glass beads: violet, gold, blue
- Candlestick with candle

Foil from Amaco; wire from Artistic Wire.

Project Notes

Refer to quarter-patterns throughout. Stylus used to create "embossed" designs on collars should not be so sharp that it tears the foil.

Violet Collar

1. For each candle collar, cut one each of violet patterns A and B from violet foil using scissors. Cut out center holes using craft knife, adjusting openings to fit candle.

2. Emboss patterns on foil collars by "drawing" lines with stylus.

3. Using stylus, carefully perforate small holes on Pattern A piece where indicated.

4. Cut 16 pieces of wire 2"–3" long. Fold end of each piece around gold bead; coil wire around knitting needle and add violet bead. Insert remaining end of wire through hole in foil collar and fold end on other side to hold wire in place; wires should hang from violet side. Repeat with remaining pieces of wire.

5. Place beaded collar on candlestick, violet side up; place smaller collar on top, violet sides facing. Insert candle. Fold up every other "petal" on top collar toward candle; fold down each petal on lower collar.

6. Add beads to 2" length of wire; curl around pencil, then wrap around base of candle.

Mint Collar

1. Repeat steps 1 and 2 as for violet collar, substituting mint foil and patterns C and D.

2. Place larger collar (C) on candlestick, mint side up; place smaller collar on top, mint side up. Insert candle. Fold down each petal on lower collar. ✂

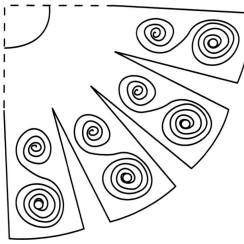

Violet A

Violet B

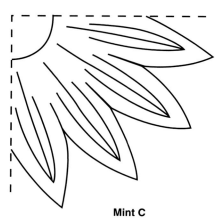

Mint C

Mint D

Kaleidoscope Candle Holder

This candle holder's true beauty comes to light when it is lit and allowed to glow in the dark. Sprays of light radiate in each direction, like a colorful kaleidoscope.

Design by Debba Haupert

Materials

- Aluminum mesh*
- 3½"-tall, 3¼"-diameter columnar glass candle holder
- Approximately 60 glass drops in desired color(s)
- 26-gauge tinned copper (silver) wire*

Amaco WireForm Diamond Aluminum Mesh; wire from Artistic Wire.

Instructions

1. *Base:* Note measurements of candle holder. Cut aluminum mesh 1" wider than candle holder's height and 1" longer than its circumference at widest point. Fold under ½" of mesh along top and bottom. Wrap mesh around votive. Holding mesh ends together, fold over ½", then another ½" to tightly secure mesh around candle holder.

2. Cut several strips of mesh 1½" x 20" (number needed will depend on size of candle holder).

3. Place first glass drop under mesh about 2" from one end with front of drop touching mesh. Fold top and bottom edges of mesh over bead (they will overlap slightly in back). Twist length of mesh once to hold drop in place; position another glass drop face up under mesh ½" from first and twist again so that both drops have the overlap in the back, a twist in between, and are face up.

4. Continue adding beads until you reach last 2" of mesh strip; then, overlap end over end of a second strip and continue (overlapped portion will be secured by twisting). Continue until you have a "rope" of glass drops encased in mesh sufficient to coil around candle holder and cover it.

5. Cut 24" wire. Beginning at top of seam on votive, insert wire into end of mesh and seam. Slip end of wire through base mesh and end of mesh rope; twist to fasten and leave end untrimmed.

6. Tightly coil mesh rope of glass beads around candle holder to cover it. Leave 1½" of mesh at end of rope to insert in base at bottom.

7. Using end of wire attached in step 5, sew down seam, attaching each row of rope as you do so. Sew bottom row of glass drops around bottom of mesh base for added strength. Twist wire end tightly; clip excess and fold under base of candle holder. ✂

Tulips & Plaid Votive

As fresh as springtime, this painted glass candle cup glitters in sunlight or candlelight.
Adapt the colors for a whole palette of sparkling beauties!

Design by Betsy H. Edwards

Materials

- Clear glass flowerpot candle holder
- Enamel paints*: ultra white, light peach, true green
- Paintbrushes: 10/0 liner, #5 round, #4 flat
- Surface conditioner*
- Paint thinner/dilutant*
- Tracing paper and pencil
- Clear tape
- 1 package apricot quartz gel candle*
- Gel candle wicks*
- Candle scent*
- Paper towels

PermEnamel paints, surface conditioner and thinner/dilutant, and Delta Gel Candle, wicks and scent, all from Delta.

Painting

1. Wash votive; rinse and dry. Paint exterior of votive with surface conditioner. (If you leave project unpainted for more than 4 hours, you will need to reapply surface conditioner.)

2. Referring to patterns throughout, trace two of each flower onto tracing paper; cut apart and tape inside votive.

3. *Paint flowers on outside of votive:* Using round brush, paint petals peach and leaves green. Thin green with a little thinner; using liner, paint stems.

4. Thin white; use to outline petals and add tiny comma-stroke highlights.

5. *Paint rim of flowerpot:* Using flat brush, paint white stripe around top edge of rim and another around bottom edge. Let dry, then add second coat.

6. Using flat brush, paint vertical green and white stripes alternately around rim, leaving unpainted stripes in between. Complete "plaid" pattern by adding vertical and horizontal lines of thinned white, green and peach with liner.

Candle

1. Following manufacturer's instructions throughout, melt candle gel and add scent as directed.

2. Place drop of melted gel in center bottom of votive; press wick anchor into gel and hold until set—about 15 seconds. Pour melted candle gel into votive to within ¾" of top. Let set.

3. Trim wick ¼" above gel. ✂

Tulips & Plaid Votive

Tin-Can Candle Holder

Who would guess this pretty painted candle holder began as a discarded tin can? Make a bunch for your picnic table or mantel.

Design by Paula Bales

Materials

- 3¼"-tall x 3¼"-diameter recycled tin can, top and label removed, cleaned and dried
- Metal paints*: baby pink, cornflower blue, bright white, sage green
- Paintbrushes: #12 shader, #0 round
- Straight pin
- Black fine-line marker*
- 16" cotton candy blue 24-gauge wire*
- 2¾"-tall x 3"-diameter candle

DecoArt No-Prep Metal Paints; ZIG Memory System Millennium MSO8 pure black marker from EK Success Ltd.; Fun Wire from Toner Plastics.

Instructions

1. Paint can pink inside and out; let dry. Use tip of brush handle to dot on white paint; let dry.

2. Referring to instructions for "Using Transfer & Graphite Paper" in the General Instructions, page 174, transfer pattern onto sides of can. Retrace pattern with marker.

3. Paint grass, stems and leaves green. Paint flowers blue with pink centers; let dry, then dot each center with white. Dot clusters of three blue dots randomly onto grass using head of straight pin.

4. Touch up outlines with marker.

5. Wrap wire around rim of can; bend into a bow. ✂

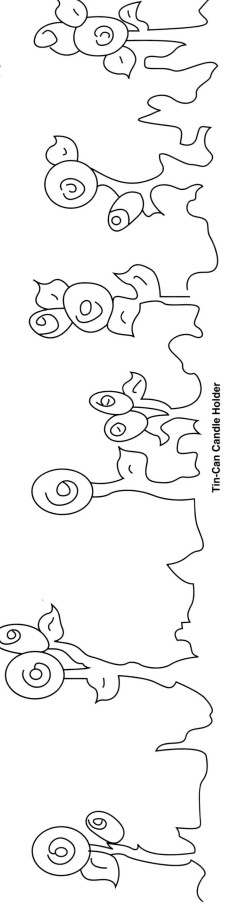

Tin-Can Candle Holder

Practice Makes Perfect!

Using scraps to practice your skills and new techniques is a great way to use up leftovers from any craft. Rather than make a mistake on a project, make the mistake on the scrap!

I love to rubber-stamp on leather; however, the ink color I select often doesn't have the same hue once I've stamped it. So I created a color chart of my inks on leather scraps so I'm not surprised by color changes. The same idea can be used for any crafting technique, from calligraphy to quilting.

Use scraps of paper to practice:
- brush strokes
- shading and highlighting
- letter spacing
- drawing or sketching
- weaving patterns

Use scraps of fabric or felt to practice and/or test:
- French knots
- painting
- sewing machine setup and tension settings
- new embroidery stitches
- glue bonding

Loving Lessons
Jelly Bean Jars

These are sure to be big hits with anyone lucky enough to receive one! Personalize the message as you wish … include jelly beans in school colors or favorite flavors … the options are endless!

Designs by Bev George

Materials
- Jar with lid
- Jelly beans
- Glue: tacky craft glue and white school glue

Decorating options
- Polymer clay: red, green, yellow, orange, black, white, pink, blue, purple
- Cookie sheet
- Oven
- Acrylic paints: red, green, yellow, orange, black, white, pink, blue, purple
- Small, white, jelly-bean-shaped dried beans
- Paintbrush
- Masking tape
- Oven-shrink plastic sheets
- Permanent felt-tip markers or paint pens
- Hole punch
- 22-gauge wire: silver and assorted colors as desired
- Assorted beads, charms
- Vellum or parchment
- Decorative ¼" ribbon or floss

Instructions

Fill jar with jelly beans. Decorate as desired using any of the following options:

Mold jelly bean from each color clay, rolling colors into ¼" rolls and slicing off ¾" section for each bean. Mold also a base from desired color(s) to fit top of lid. Following manufacturer's instructions, bake beans and base; let cool. Using tacky glue, glue jelly beans to base and base to lid.

Paint dried white beans to resemble jelly beans or color them with markers (secure them on masking tape, if desired); let dry. Touch up bare spots; let dry. Glue beans to lid using tacky glue. Seal by brushing a coat of white school glue over beans.

Make shrink-plastic jelly beans, following manufacturer's instructions for working with plastic and referring to patterns; cut small shape for each color and large one for poem or other message. Outline small beans and add color names with colored pens. Use black marker to write "is for Joy," "is for Faithfulness," etc., on smaller beans, and poem or other message on larger bean. Punch hole in shapes and bake as directed. Coil silver wire around pencil or straw; wrap around neck of bottle. Suspend plastic jelly beans from wire using

○

Small Jelly Bean

○

Large Jelly Bean

silver or colored wire, adding charms or beads as desired.

Or, wrap neck of jar with colored ribbon or floss and suspend jelly bean shapes.

Write poem or message on small piece of vellum or parchment; roll into scroll and tie with ribbon or floss; tie to jelly bean jar. ✄

A jar of jelly beans so colorful and sweet;
The fruits of the Spirit, a loved one's treat.

Red	**Orange**	**Pink**
is for Love	is for Goodness	is for Joy
Green	**Black**	**Blue**
is for Gentleness	is for Self-Control	is for Kindness
Yellow	**White**	**Purple**
is for Patience	is for Peace	is for Faithfulness

Springtime Bunny Buddy

Peeking out from a watering can, this sweet bunny brings seasonal greetings and a bouquet of color.

Design by Ginny Baker

Materials

- 2" metal watering can
- Aluminum foil
- Polymer clay*: tan, blue, dusty rose, lavender, lemon, white, emerald green
- Small paintbrush
- Pink chalk
- ¼" flower shape cutter* (optional)
- Craft knife
- Needle tool
- 2 (1¹⁄₁₆") black ball head pins
- Wire cutters
- 3" thin brown craft wire
- 1½" x ½" balsa wood
- Fine-tip black marker
- Plain white paper
- Baking sheet
- Ruler or circle template
- Oven
- White tacky glue
- Toothpicks
- Acrylic paints: white, yellow

Sculpey III polymer clay from Polyform; Kemper shape cutter.

Project Note

Refer to manufacturer's instructions for working with polymer clay and using shape cutter.

Instructions

1. Fill watering can to within 1" of top with crumpled aluminum foil; flatten 1" ball of green clay and cover with foil.

2. *Bunny body:* Roll 1½" ball tan clay into cone; place in center of watering can.

3. *Arms:* Roll two ¾" balls tan clay into tapered logs; press tapered ends to sides of body. Using needle tool, impress claw marks in paws.

4. *Head:* Break toothpick in half; insert end into top of body. Roll ¾" ball tan clay into rounded cone; press gently onto other end of toothpick. Rub paintbrush across chalk; lightly blush cheeks.

5. *Muzzle, mouth and nose:* Roll ⁵⁄₁₆" ball white clay; flatten slightly and press onto lower center of face. Make mouth opening with toothpick. Roll two ¼" balls white; flatten slightly and press over mouth. Shape ⅛" ball dusty rose into triangle; press into space between muzzles.

6. *Eyes:* Cut heads from pins and press into face on either side of nose; indent eyelashes with needle tool.

7. *Ears:* Roll two ½" balls tan into tapered logs; flatten gently. Repeat with two ⅜" balls dusty rose for ear centers; press into center of each ear. Make fur marks around edges of dusty rose centers with needle tool.

8. *Flowers:* Use flower cutter to cut flowers from flattened blue, dusty rose and lavender clay; add tiny yellow ball in center of each. Or, roll ¼" balls blue, dusty rose and lavender into teardrops for petals; press tapered ends of petals together to form flowers; press tiny yellow balls in centers. Make leaves from small green teardrops indented with needle tool; position with flowers in front of and behind bunny.

9. *Sign:* Insert wire into green clay behind bunny; press small, flattened scrap of tan clay onto top end of wire. Use marker to write "SPRING IS IN THE AIR!" on balsa rectangle; set aside till piece is baked. Make small lavender flower with yellow center to affix to sign later.

10. *Heart:* Shape ⅜" ball dusty rose clay into teardrop; indent rounded end with needle tool to make heart.

11. *Baking:* Place white paper on baking sheet; set watering can, lavender flower and heart on paper and bake in preheated 265-degree oven for 40 minutes. Let cool completely.

12. *Assembly:* Glue lavender flower to sign and sign to clay at top of wire; glue heart to front of watering can.

13. *Painting:* Using toothpick, dot tiny white flowers with yellow centers around base of watering can; add tiny white highlights to eyes. ✂

SPRING IS IN THE AIR!

Instructions for
Easter Egg Candle
Cup begin on
next page.

Easter Egg Candle Cup

You'll enjoy decorating a discarded tin can with pastel Easter eggs fashioned from polymer clay!
If candles aren't your style, fill it with a nest of Easter grass and sweet treats!

Design by Ginny Baker

Materials

- Soft polymer clay*: pastel lemon, pastel mint, pastel raspberry, pastel orchid, pastel sky blue
- Clean, empty 3-ounce tuna can with pull-off top
- Rolling pin or acrylic brayer
- Splash pattern dotter tool*
- Shape cutters* (optional): ³⁄₁₆" and ³⁄₈" hearts, ³⁄₁₆" and ³⁄₈" flowers
- Craft knife
- Needle tool
- Plain white paper
- Baking sheet
- Ruler or circle template
- Oven

Fimo Soft polymer clay from Amaco; Fun to Paint Splash dotter tool from Plaid; Kemper shape cutters.

Project Notes

Refer to manufacturer's instructions for working with polymer clay and using shape cutters. Never use a rolling pin that has been used on polymer clay for food preparation.

Instructions

1. Flatten 2-ounce package of lemon clay ⅛" thick; cut 5" x 1" rectangle and wrap around sides of can. Trim off excess so ends butt neatly and trim excess along top and bottom. Rub seam gently with finger to smooth.

2. Randomly imprint clay using splash dotter.

3. Roll 1" ball sky blue, 1" ball mint, 1" ball orchid and 1" ball raspberry; shape each into egg shape.

4. *Sky blue egg:* Cut seven tiny triangles from ¹⁄₁₆"-thick raspberry clay; affix in two rows, at top (three triangles) and bottom (four), points toward center. Roll two thin ropes orchid; attach one at base of each row. Roll tiny balls of lemon; position between triangles. Cut ³⁄₁₆"

heart from ¹⁄₁₆"-thick orchid clay; press in center of egg.

5. *Mint egg:* Cut five ³⁄₁₆" flowers from ¹⁄₁₆"-thick raspberry clay and five from ¹⁄₁₆" orchid. (If not using cutter, roll ⅛" balls of clay; flatten each and indent edges with needle tool to simulate petals.) Affix in two rows, at top and bottom, alternating colors. Cut ³⁄₁₆" heart from ¹⁄₁₆"-thick lemon clay; press in center of egg.

6. *Orchid egg:* Roll thin ropes of mint, raspberry, blue and lemon. Starting at top of egg, attach mint, then raspberry ropes, trimming excess. Leave ½" in center of egg, then affix blue and lemon ropes. Use needle tool to add texture to each rope. Roll tiny dots of all four colors and attach to egg in center.

7. *Raspberry egg:* Roll thin 2" rope of mint; cut in half and affix one across top half of egg and one across bottom half in scalloped pattern. Cut ⅜" flower from ¹⁄₁₆"-thick orchid clay; attach to center of egg and press tiny lemon ball in center. Use needle tool to add detail down center of petals. (If not using cutter, roll five ⅛" balls orchid and shape into teardrops; flatten slightly for petals and attach lemon ball in center.)

8. *Hearts:* Cut ⅜" heart from ¹⁄₁₆"-thick orchid, blue, raspberry and mint clays; affix to side of can between eggs. (Or form hearts by hand, forming ⅜" ball of each color into teardrop and indenting tops with needle tool.)

9. *Baking:* Place white paper on baking sheet; set candle cup on paper and bake in preheated 265-degree oven for 30 minutes. Let cool completely before handling. ✁

Baby Love Bath Set

Bargain-basement washcloths and crafting odds and ends combine to make a pair of sweet bath-time buddies! Add simple homemade soaps for a truly memorable baby gift.

Designs by Marilyn Gossett

Materials

Bunny & Chick

- Terrycloth washcloths: light pink, light yellow
- Felt: white, orange
- Pompoms: 2 (½") white, 1" white, 7mm pink
- 4 (⅛") black half-round eyes
- 1⅛ yards ¼"-wide blue gingham ribbon
- ½" ribbon roses: yellow, pink
- Powdered blush
- Cotton-tip swab
- Fiberfill
- Sewing needle and thread
- Glue

Soaps

- Soap*: white, clear, dark blue chunks
- Soap dye: red, blue
- Soap fragrance of your choice
- Soap molds*: 2½" square, 2¾" heart, 2½" x 3½" rectangle
- 2 (1") heart candy molds
- Clear polyester glitter
- 3 clear cellophane bags
- 12" ¼"-wide satin ribbon: pink, yellow, blue
- Wooden craft sticks
- Spoon
- Microwavable measuring cup
- Sharp, smooth knife
- Rubbing alcohol in a spray bottle

Life of the Party soap; Soap Creations molds from Delta.

Bunny

1. Lay pink washcloth wrong side up. Fold sides to center so edges meet (Figs. 1 and 2). Fold in half again (Fig. 3).

2. Fold rectangle in half from top to bottom, matching short edges. Stitch or pin short edges together.

3. Tie 15" piece of ribbon around neck 2" below top fold; tie ribbon in shoestring bow with 1" loops and 2" tails; trim ends at an angle.

4. Cut ears on fold from white felt; thread ears through head loop and gather together on top of head with a 6-inch length of ribbon; tie in bow. Blush cheeks and inner ears with powdered blush and cotton swab.

5. Glue two eyes to face; add smaller white pompoms for muzzle and pink pompom for nose. Glue yellow rose to center of neck bow; glue larger white pompom to back of bunny for tail.

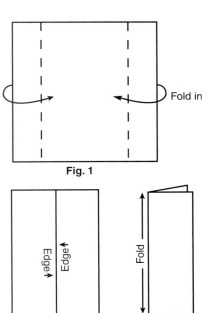

Fold in

Fig. 1

Fig. 2

Edge

Edge

Fig. 3

Fold

Fold

Bunny Ears
Cut 1 on fold from white felt

Chick

1. Lay yellow washcloth wrong side up. Place 2" ball of fiberfill in center; pull washcloth edges down, right side facing out. Push fiberfill in with finger and shape into round head with your other hand.

2. Tie 15" piece of ribbon around base of head in shoestring bow with 1½" loops and 2" tails; trim ends at an angle.

3. Place a larger ball of fiberfill in washcloth; smooth down front (chest). Pull edges of washcloth to back; smooth and tie 12" piece of ribbon in small bow at base of tail. Smooth and fluff edges of washcloth to form tail feathers.

Chick Beak
Cut 1 from orange felt

4. Cut beak from orange felt; fold in half and glue fold to face; glue on eyes. Blush cheeks with cosmetic blush and cotton swab. Glue pink rose to center of neck bow.

Basic Instructions for Making Soaps

When measuring soaps, note that 12 (1") *cubes of soap will equal 1 cup melted soap.*

Melting and molding soap: Cut soap into 1" cubes. Microwave in measuring cup on HIGH for 30 seconds; stir with craft stick, then heat for additional 5-second intervals until melted. *Do not pour if soap is steaming.* Using craft stick, stir in soap dye one drop at a time. Add fragrance; pour into mold. Spritz with rubbing alcohol to remove bubbles. Set molded soap in freezer for about 10 minutes before removing soap from mold; it will pop out easily.

Confetti: Pour colored soap into any flat mold; let set. Cut into irregular ¼" and ½" chunks.

Add confetti to soap: Place confetti chunks in freezer for 10 minutes to harden before adding to base soap to prevent melting.

Soaps

1. *Pink heart:* Melt 1 cup white soap cubes. Add a pinch of glitter, 1 drop red dye (or more as needed) and fragrance. Pour into 2¾" heart mold; also pour some into heart candy mold for rectangular soap. Spritz with alcohol and let set. Pop out of molds.

2. *Pink square:* Pour remaining melted pink soap into square mold; add a drop of blue dye to small amount of melted pink soap; pour into candy mold. Let set and pop out of molds.

3. *Blue rectangle:* Follow basic instructions to make dark blue soap confetti. Cut 1" clear soap cube into smaller chunks for confetti.

4. Melt 6 cubes white soap. Add one drop blue dye. Stir in dye and fragrance. Pour melted soap into mold, filling it halfway. Add soap confetti; spritz with alcohol. Let set for a couple of minutes before filling mold with remaining melted soap. Spritz with alcohol. Let set; pop out of mold.

5. *Attach hearts:* Pop pink and blue hearts from candy molds. Melt one cube clear soap without overheating it. Place a small dollop of clear soap in middle of pink square; place blue heart on dollop; let set. Repeat, adding pink heart to blue confetti soap.

6. Place each bar of soap in cellophane bag; tie closed with ribbon bow. Or, wrap each bar in plastic wrap to prevent condensation; hold wrap closed with a pretty sticker. ✄

Organizing Your Scraps

If you are a pack rat like most crafters, it's almost painful to throw out scraps of any kind, from felt bits to odds and ends of paper. Here are a few tips for helping you keep your scraps from taking over your craft area.

• Use see-through containers whenever possible. Using clear plastic boxes, glass jars or self-sealing bags lets you know at a glance what you have. Any opaque container should be clearly labeled on the outside.

• Great scrap organizers include tackle boxes, multidrawer miniature cabinets, over-the-door plastic pocket organizers (used most often for jewelry or shoes by non-crafters), sectional plastic boxes and baby-food jars.

• Store materials by color. Most of us craft by color theme, so it's logical to organize that way. You can also organize by size within the color family.

• Keep like items together. For example, if you like to make jewelry, keep scraps of threads, beads and other like supplies in one container. You'll have the supplies to make a craft project all organized without much effort.

• Using a scrap of paper, make a note of when the scrap was placed in a container. If the scrap isn't used within a year, consider donating it to a school or community program. This keeps the dust levels down!

Springtime Floor Mat

Salvage a scrap of vinyl flooring or a discarded showroom sample to paint this durable, colorful floor mat.

Design by June Fiechter

Materials

- 18" x 24" vinyl flooring
- Outdoor paints*: sunshine yellow, pine green, summer sky blue, cloud white, geranium red, golden honey, wrought iron black, clear coat
- Cellulose sponge
- Large foam brush
- ⅜" paintbrush

Patio Paints from DecoArt.

Project Notes

Use photocopier to enlarge pattern 150 percent.

Wrong side of flooring will be the right side of painted floor mat. Leave a thin, even, unpainted border between painted rectangles to create the look of tiles. Let paints dry and clean cellulose sponge and brush between coats.

Instructions

1. Using foam brush, paint wrong side of vinyl flooring white.

2. Pencil two rectangular borders around mat, one 4" in from edge and another 5" from edge.

3. Dampen cellulose sponge; wring out until nearly dry. Mix 1 part red with 5 parts clear coat; dip corner of sponge into mixture and smear, pat, rub and push paint in outermost border, creating "veins" with edge of sponge.

4. Using ⅜" brush, add marble lines

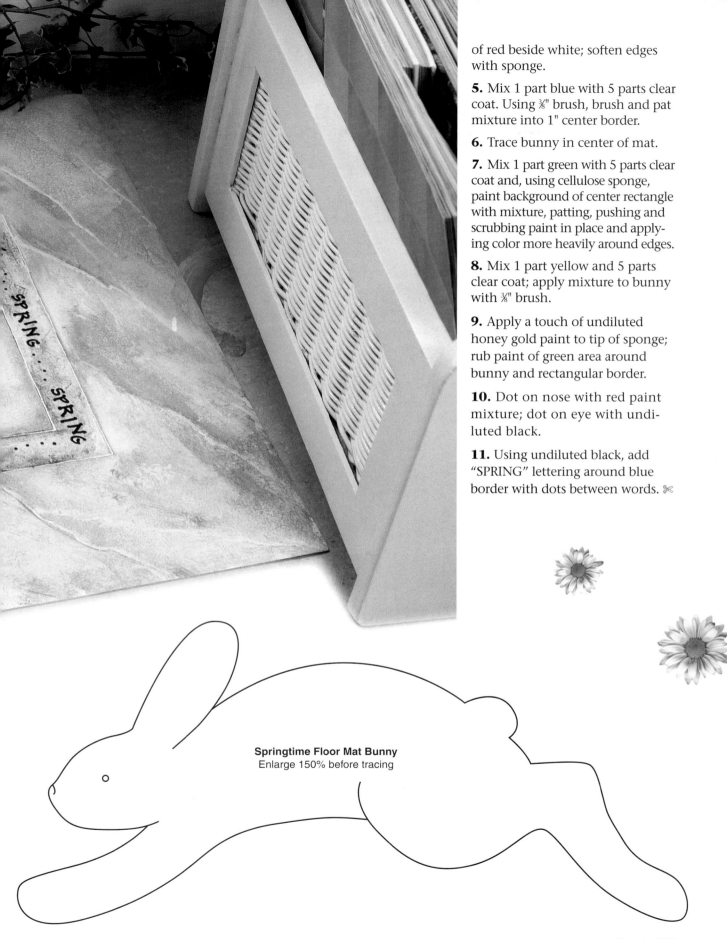

of red beside white; soften edges with sponge.

5. Mix 1 part blue with 5 parts clear coat. Using ⅜" brush, brush and pat mixture into 1" center border.

6. Trace bunny in center of mat.

7. Mix 1 part green with 5 parts clear coat and, using cellulose sponge, paint background of center rectangle with mixture, patting, pushing and scrubbing paint in place and applying color more heavily around edges.

8. Mix 1 part yellow and 5 parts clear coat; apply mixture to bunny with ⅜" brush.

9. Apply a touch of undiluted honey gold paint to tip of sponge; rub paint of green area around bunny and rectangular border.

10. Dot on nose with red paint mixture; dot on eye with undiluted black.

11. Using undiluted black, add "SPRING" lettering around blue border with dots between words. ✂

Springtime Floor Mat Bunny
Enlarge 150% before tracing

Springtime Button Babe

Use up all kinds of crafting notions to create this magical miss!

She bears a very special gift: a basket of springtime!

Design by Lorine Mason

Materials

- Wooden plaques: 4" heart, 4" rectangle
- ¼" dowels: 2 (4"), 1"
- 1½" wooden doll head knob
- Drill with ¼" bit
- 3" straw hat
- Craft foam: white, beige
- 2 yards green plastic-coated 24-gauge wire
- 3" crocheted doily
- 2 (1") feather butterflies on wire stems
- 8" ⅛"-wide turquoise ribbon
- Paintbrush
- Acrylic paints*: Indian turquoise, white, baby pink, flesh tone, black
- Toothpick
- Satin-finish varnish
- 1½"–2" basket
- Assorted small shank buttons
- Black extra-fine-point permanent marker
- Floral foam
- Dried Spanish moss
- 3"–4" silk flower
- Seagull decorative paper edgers*
- Hot-glue gun

Americana acrylic paints from DecoArt; Fiskars paper edgers.

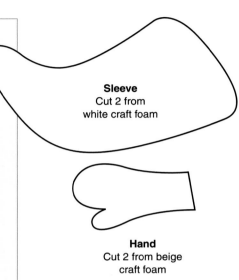

Sleeve
Cut 2 from white craft foam

Hand
Cut 2 from beige craft foam

Instructions

1. Find center of rectangular plaque; measure out ½" from each side of center and mark; drill ⅜"-deep hole at each mark. Drill matching holes in center of heart plaque's curved edge. Drill single hole in edge of heart at point.

2. Paint all surfaces of heart turquoise; paint top of rectangle white and beveled edges and bottom turquoise; let dry. Using brush handle dipped in pink, dot spots onto white surface.

3. Paint doll head flesh tone; paint all dowels white; let dry.

4. Apply two coats varnish to all painted pieces; let dry.

5. Referring to photo throughout, dot eyes onto doll head with brush handle dipped in white; let dry. Add black pupils, then tiny white highlights using toothpick. Rouge cheeks with fingertip dipped in pink. Add eyebrows, nose and smile with extra-fine-point marker; add tiny white highlight dots at ends of smile and each cheek.

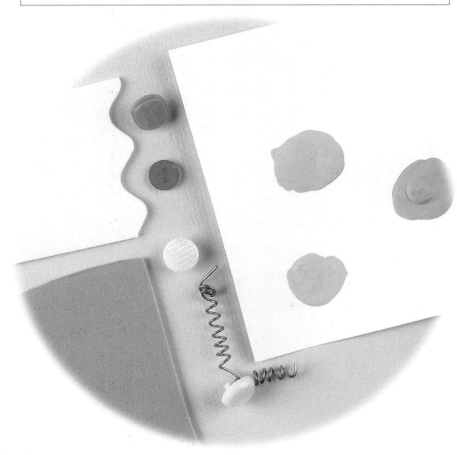

6. Cut two hands from beige craft foam and two sleeves from white; trim sleeves' cuff ends with paper edgers.

7. Weave ribbon through two holes in doily near center; tie in a bow; trim ends.

8. Glue head onto 1" dowel; poke dowel through center of doily; apply a drop of glue to end and insert dowel in hole at point of heart.

9. Glue hat to back of head. Cut apart silk flower; trim petals to fit around edge of hat. Starting at back of head, glue petals around edge of face in rows, using largest petals in first row and smaller petals closer to face.

10. Cut nine 6" pieces of wire. Form each into a button flower: Thread shank button onto wire to center, then twist wires together about ½"; leave one end straight for stem and coil other around brush handle and bend up for leaf. Repeat to make nine flowers.

11. Cut foam to fit in basket; glue in place. Glue Spanish moss over surface. Arrange six flowers and a butterfly in basket, applying dot of glue to ends of stem wires before inserting in foam.

12. Glue hands to bottoms of sleeves; glue sleeves at top of heart plaque. Glue hands to sides of basket, holding in place until glue sets.

13. Apply dot of glue to each end of remaining dowels; insert one end in bottom of body and other end in top of rectangle.

14. Cut two 12" pieces wire. Beginning at top of leg, wrap one piece down and around it, leaving 5" at end. Thread this end through button shank, leaving 1½" stem; bend wire and twist together. Coil free end around brush handle and bend up. Repeat on other leg.

15. Glue Spanish moss at base of legs; glue on remaining button flowers and butterfly; glue a few buttons without stems directly to moss. ✀

Birds, Bugs & Bees

The painting is simple and fast, but the results are delightful!
Whip up this wall hanging for kitchen or sunroom in next to no time!

Design by Jodie Bushman for Delta Technical Coatings

Materials

- 10½" x 10¼" section rustic picket fence
- 4 wooden birdhouses*
- Wooden cutouts*: 19 (⅜") circles, 5 (1") ovals, 16 (⅞") teardrops
- 2 (1½") wooden watering cans
- ⅝" ribbon roses on stems: 5 each of 2 colors
- 12" natural raffia
- Acrylic paints* bungalow blue, opaque red, alpine green, light chocolate, buttercream, raspberry, black, white, opaque yellow
- Driftwood pickling gel*
- Matte-finish interior/exterior varnish*
- Tacky glue
- Paintbrushes: #0 liner, #8 shader
- Masking tape
- Stylus

Chunky birdhouses from Darice; Woodsies cutouts from Forster; Ceramcoat acrylic paints, Home Décor Pickling Gel and Matte Interior/Exterior varnish, all from Delta.

Instructions

1. Brush all surfaces of fence with pickling gel; let dry.

2. Glue together four left-facing birds, gluing circle (head) and teardrop (wing) atop another teardrop (body). Make two right-facing birds in the same manner. Make one bird with two wings, gluing circle (head) to end of oval, and two other teardrops on back (broad ends facing) for wings.

3. Glue together three bees, gluing two circles (wings) side by side in middle of oval (body).

4. Mount small wooden pieces on sticky side of masking tape to hold them for painting. Base-coat as follows (refer to "Painting Techniques" in the General Instructions, page 174): *blue*—birds and one birdhouse; *red*—remaining circles; *green*—one birdhouse; *chocolate*—one birdhouse; *buttercream*—one birdhouse and one watering can; *raspberry*—one watering can; *white*—bees' wings; *yellow*—bees' bodies.

5. Add details using liner brush and dotting on paints with stylus:

Birds—Add white highlight strokes to wing and tiny white specks to chest; dot on yellow beaks and black eyes; when dry, add tiny white highlights to eyes.

Ladybugs—Add black line down center of back; dot on black spots.

Bees—Add black lines to wings and stripes to bodies; dot on black eyes.

Birdhouses—Dot white around openings of all but buttercream birdhouse; paint front of buttercream birdhouse roof green.

Watering cans—Paint green band around buttercream can and buttercream band around raspberry can.

6. Apply varnish to all pieces; let dry.

7. Glue painted pieces onto fence. Paint black dashed "trails" between ladybugs; dot black heads onto fence next to ladybugs. Glue stems of roses in watering cans. Cut raffia in half; loop each half through hole in side of fence. ✄

Blooming Birdhouses Denim Shirt

Fabric paints in soft iridescent hues make a beautiful springtime topper.

Design by Bev Shenefield

Materials

- Denim shirt
- 3D fabric paints*: golden yellow iridescent, white mist iridescent, watermelon
- Fabric dyes*: black, English yew, starlite white
- Paintbrushes: flat and liner
- Chalk pencil and/or transfer paper
- Shirt-painting board
- Black fine-point permanent marker

Scribbles 3D Soft Fashion Paints from Duncan; Delta fabric dyes.

Project Note

Refer to pattern (page 42) throughout. Use a photocopier to enlarge pattern 182 percent before reproducing it on shirt.

Instructions

1. Wash and dry shirt without using fabric softener; press.

2. Using chalk pencil and referring to "Using Transfer and Graphite Paper" in the General Instructions, page 174, transfer enlarged pattern onto right front of shirt. Place shirt-painting board inside shirt under pattern area.

3. Paint birdhouses and posts white mist. Paint roof on taller birdhouse golden yellow; paint other roof with a mixture of white mist and watermelon.

4. Using flat brush, add plaid pattern to taller birdhouse using watermelon/white mist mixture for horizontal lines and golden yellow for vertical lines. Using liner and English yew, add double rows of horizontal and vertical lines.

5. Using flat brush, add plaid pattern to shorter birdhouse using watermelon/white mist mixture for vertical lines and golden yellow for horizontal lines. Using liner and English yew, add single rows of horizontal and vertical lines.

6. Paint squiggly lines along roofs with starlite white; paint birdhouse openings black.

7. Paint leaves and stems English yew; highlight with golden yellow.

8. Paint centers of two tulips golden yellow; paint outer petals with watermelon/white mist mixture. Reverse color scheme on remaining tulips.

9. Using liner, add plaid pattern to outer petals, using watermelon/white mist mixture on golden yellow petals and golden yellow on watermelon/white mist petals.

10. Use fine-point marker to outline and add details to birdhouses, posts, tulips, stems and leaves. ✄

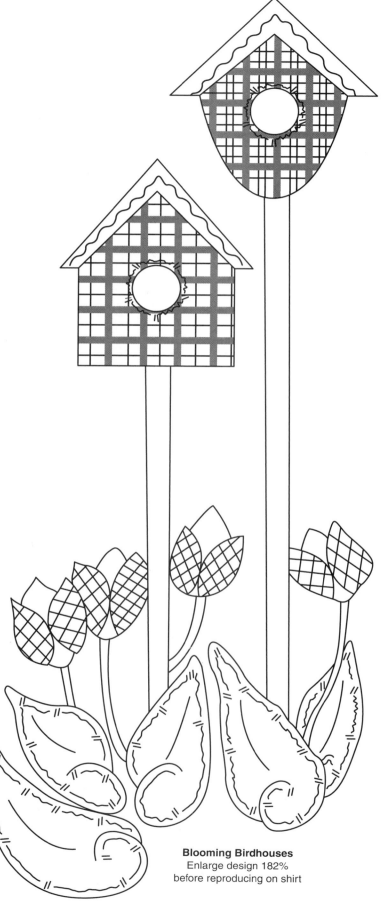

Blooming Birdhouses
Enlarge design 182%
before reproducing on shirt

Blue Poppies Hat

*Whether you make this hat to wear or simply to dress up a guest room
or vintage hat rack, you'll enjoy the splash of color from its silk blooms.*

Design by Bev Shenefield

Materials

- Natural straw hat
- 6 light blue silk poppies with leaves
- ⅔ yard 1"-wide light blue moiré ribbon
- Hot-glue gun

Instructions

1. Hot-glue ribbon around crown of hat, overlapping ends in front.

2. Hot-glue poppies and leaves to crown and brim on front of hat, concealing ribbon ends. ✄

Chenille-Edged Pillowcases

The plainest of pillowcases take on designer flair with the addition of super-simple chenille trims.

Design by Fran Rohus

Materials

- 2 standard pillowcases
- Transfer or graphite paper
- Chenille trim*: 100 inches grape soda, 20 inches limeade, 20 inches blueberry, 10 inches raspberry
- Chenille cutting guide*
- Chenille brush*
- Needle and matching sewing threads
- Spray bottle filled with water

Chenille by the Inch, Chenille Brush and Chenille Cutting Guide, all from Fabric Café.

Chenille-Edged Pillowcases
Enlarge pattern 200% before transferring

COLOR KEY
—— Grape soda
○ Raspberry
—— Limeade
—— Blueberry

Project Notes

Refer to pattern throughout; enlarge pattern 200 percent before transferring pattern to fabric.

Instructions

1. Referring to instructions for "Using Transfer and Graphite Paper" in the General Instructions (page 174), transfer design to edge of pillowcase opening, centering it 1" from open edge.

2. Remove tear-away backing from chenille trim; cut into long strips using cutting guide.

3. Sew strips to pillowcase, back-tacking at beginning and end of each strip.

4. Brush chenille with chenille brush, spraying it lightly with water as you brush. Launder pillowcases to enhance the fluff. ✄

Quilting Gone Crazy

From its humble roots in years gone by, "crazy quilting" has evolved into a delightful art form that cries out to scrap crafters!

Every quilter lives by the credo that "she with the most fabric wins." Keeping every scrap of fabric is a perfect habit for this art and craft. During the Victorian age, "crazy quilting" was a favored pastime. A crazy quilt is made up of randomly pieced fabrics finished with fancy embroidery along most of the seams.

However, the true art of the crazy quilt was perfected by our foremothers in Colonial America, where "crazy quilting" was practiced for frugal reasons rather than artistic expression. What appeared to be a coverlet of randomly pieced odds and ends was in fact a crucial money-saving measure. When a blanket began to wear out, savvy sewers patched it with any fabric at hand. Over time, these imaginative, thrifty and creative women brought beauty to even the scrap rags used for patching by adding elaborate stitching. It seems that even our ancestors were into scrap crafting!

Scraps of fabric are also wonderful for patchwork quilts, lap quilts, baby quilts and miniature quilts. It's best to wash the fabric before cutting, and always iron the scraps before storing.

"Crazy Quilt" Boxes

Have a ball dabbing vibrant colors onto the lids of heart-shaped boxes to transform them into delightful little tree boxes! They're the perfect holders for treats and tiny gifts of all kinds.

Design by Mary Ayres

Materials

Both Boxes

- 2 (3") heart-shaped papier-mâché boxes with lids*
- Wooden cutouts*: 2 (⅞") stars, 2 (½" x 1") rectangles
- 2 (½") flat brown buttons
- Acrylic paints*: petal pink, royal fuchsia, baby blue, Victorian blue, sea aqua, deep teal, Indian turquoise, desert turquoise, summer lilac, lavender, raspberry, cranberry wine, olde gold, milk chocolate, soft black
- Glorious gold metallic acrylic paint*
- Texture finger mitts*: rag, mop, chamois
- Markers*: black fine-tip, extra-fine-tip opaque gold
- Thick white glue*
- Paintbrushes

Boxes from D&CC; Forster Woodsies wood shapes; Americana and Dazzling Metallics paints from DecoArt; ZIG Memory System permanent markers from EK Success Ltd.; Fun to Paint Texture Finger Mitts from Plaid; Kids Choice Glue from Beacon.

Using Finger Mitts

1. Pour small amount of dabbing color on paper plate. Wet mitt with water; blot excess onto paper towel.

2. Place mitt on finger. Dip mitt in paint; blot on paper towel. Dab mitt onto painted surface until desired color is achieved.

Lavender, Turquoise & Cranberry Box

1. Paint sides and bottom of box olde gold.

2. Divide top of box lid into three sections; paint one section desert turquoise, then dab with Indian turquoise using finger mitt. Let dry.

3. Tape edge of painted section alongside next section to be painted. Paint with cranberry wine, then dab with raspberry using different finger mitt. Remove tape; let dry.

4. Tape edges of painted sections alongside remaining unpainted area. Paint lavender, then dab with lilac using third finger mitt. Remove tape; let dry.

5. Paint edges of lid black. Using gold writer, draw scallops along top edge; add vertical line through each. Draw "stitch lines" between sections on lid.

6. Paint wooden rectangle milk chocolate; draw buttonhole stitches around edges with gold marker. Paint star olde gold; draw buttonhole stitches around edge with black marker.

7. Glue star to center top of lid (tip); glue rectangle (trunk) at center bottom of lid; glue button to top of trunk.

Fuchsia, Blue & Teal Box

Follow instructions for lavender, turquoise and cranberry box, painting sections of lid fuchsia dabbed with petal pink, Victorian blue dabbed with baby blue, and deep teal dabbed with sea aqua. ✄

Jewel-Tone Mosaic Frame

A clear suction cup with a hook is just the thing for suspending
this elegant frame with the look of classical mosaic in a sunny window.

Design by E. Wayne Fox

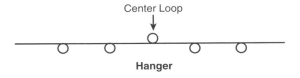

Materials

- 9" x 12" clear plastic sheet*
- Slick-surface adhesive*
- Satin varnish*
- Mosaic grout*
- ⅜" wash brush
- Drill and ³⁄₃₂" bit
- Round-nose pliers
- Wire cutters
- Masking tape
- Marbleized mosaic shapes*: rose, violet, teal
- Tinned copper wire*: 16" 20-gauge, 20" 16-gauge

K&S Engineering .030 plastic sheet; Aleene's Platinum Bond Slick Surface Adhesive; DecoArt DuraClear varnish; Clearly Mosaics grout and mosaic shapes from The Beadery; Artistic Wire.

Frame

1. Mask off 5" x 7" area in center of plastic sheet.

2. Glue mosaic shapes to frame area of plastic sheet in mosaic fashion, positioning violet shapes at top, teal in middle and rose at bottom; let dry.

3. Following manufacturer's instructions, apply grout between mosaic pieces; let dry.

4. Brush varnish over mosaic frame; let dry.

5. Drill hole ⅜" into each top corner.

Hanger

1. Cut 18" 16-gauge wire; grasp center with pliers; fold each side to opposite side to make center upright loop (see Hanger diagram).

Continued on page 50

Heart's Delight Bath Set

This entrancing collection stars a little lady whose flowered gown dresses a bottle for lotions and potions.
Fragrant bath powders and handcrafted soap complete the set.

Designs by Marilyn Gossett

Materials

Bottle Girl

- 5" heart-shaped bottle with cork stopper
- 1½" wooden ball knob
- Jumbo craft stick
- Paintbrushes: ½" angular, #0 liner
- Stylus or toothpick
- Acrylic paints*: Santa's flesh, white, black, nectar coral
- Satin-finish varnish*
- 2 (5") square white linen doilies with Battenburg edging*
- Dried Spanish moss
- 6" jute twine
- ⅔ yard ⅜"-wide pink picot-edge ribbon
- Silk flowers: 6 (½") pink rosebuds, 16 (1") sprigs lavender, 16 (1") sprigs green baby's breath, 7 (1") sprigs white baby's breath, 2 bunches ½" dark pink paper posies, 3 (1") leaves, 10 (½") burgundy and light pink rosebuds
- Sewing needle and white thread
- Hot-glue gun or tacky glue
- Extra-fine-point brown permanent marker
- Bath salts or powder

Heart Soap Slice

- Glycerin soaps: white, clear
- Microwave-safe measuring cup
- Craft sticks
- Red soap colorant

- Soap fragrance
- Small soap loaf mold
- Baking sheet
- Sharp knife
- Clear plastic wrap
- 4" x 6" red handmade paper or card stock (see Project Notes)
- ½ yard 1½"-wide sheer white ribbon
- Small flower sticker or paper cutout

Bath Powder Packet

- Clear glycerin soap
- Microwave-safe measuring cup
- Craft sticks
- Red soap colorant
- Soap fragrance
- Small heart candy mold
- Clear plastic wrap
- Decorative paper: 12" sheet light pink with dark pink lines, 3" square sheer light pink handmade paper, 3" square dark pink handmade paper or card stock (see Project Notes)
- Glue stick
- 4" x 6" plastic bag of bath salts
- Decorative paper edgers: small scallop, deckle
- 1 yard sheer white ⅞"-wide ribbon
- 1" rose sticker or cutout
- Hot-glue gun
- White adhesive-backed label
- Felt-tip pen

Ceramcoat paints from Delta; doily from Wimpole Street Creations.

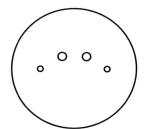

Face

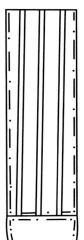

Arm

Add white stripes to sleeves with liner; add details with marker. Coat with varnish.

3. *Dress:* Fold pleat across top of doily so fold is 2¼" below top edge. Press fold against doily; sew running stitch along top of fold through both thicknesses. Pull thread ends to gather; fit around front half of bottle. Repeat with second doily to fit around back. Glue side edges of doily together, catching ends of arms in seams.

4. *Garland:* Arrange handful of Spanish moss in ropelike strand; glue along jute. Cut flower blossoms apart; arrange and glue onto

Bottle Girl

1. *Head:* Glue ball knob (head) to top of cork. Referring to patterns throughout, paint head and cork flesh; rouge cheeks with coral (see "Painting Techniques" in the General Instructions, page 174). Dot on eyes with stylus dipped in black; dot white highlight onto each cheek. Coat with varnish.

2. *Arms:* Cut craft stick in half. Paint arms coral; paint hands flesh.

Fancy Bath Pow'

moss. Glue one end of garland to each hand.

5. *Hair:* Glue small handful of Spanish moss to head. Cut 12" piece of ribbon; tie in bow and trim ends at an angle. Glue flowers and bow to Spanish moss hair.

6. Tie remaining ribbon in bow; trim tails at an angle. Glue at top of dress off to one side; glue several blossoms to bow.

7. Fill bottle with bath salts; insert cork stopper.

Heart Soap Slice

1. Cut clear soap into 1" cubes; referring to manufacturer's instructions throughout, microwave 1 cup soap cubes in measuring cup on HIGH for 33 seconds; stir with craft stick, then heat for 11-second intervals until melted. Do not allow soap to steam.

2. Pour in fragrance and red colorant, stirring thoroughly with craft stick.

3. Pour soap onto baking sheet; let harden. Trim edges to make rectangle. Roll both long sides of soap sheet toward center, forming point in center to give soap the appearance of a heart. Place in freezer for several minutes.

4. Cut white soap into 1" cubes; microwave 2 cups soap cubes in measuring cup on HIGH for 33 seconds; stir with craft stick, then heat for 11-second intervals until melted. Do not allow soap to steam.

5. Pour ½" layer of soap into mold; let cool until skin forms. Place chilled red soap on top of white soap in mold. Cut up any scraps of red soap; add to loaf.

6. Melt more white soap; stir in fragrance. Allow to cool slightly, then pour into mold until it is full. Let harden completely before popping soap from mold.

7. Cut soap into 1"-thick slices. Wrap each piece in plastic wrap.

8. Trim or tear card stock ¼" larger than soap slice all around (or, trim edges of regular card stock with decorative paper edgers). Lay wrapped slice on card stock; tie together with ribbon and finish with bow. Press flower sticker onto center of bow.

Bath Powder Packet

1. Referring to instructions for Heart Soap Slice, make a small red soap in heart candy mold; wrap in plastic wrap and glue to card stock; trim with deckle paper edgers, leaving ¼" border. Add rose sticker to center of soap.

2. Make 4" x 6" envelope from pink lined paper (or, cover 4" x 6" envelope with decorative paper); secure edges with glue stick.

3. Seal plastic bag of bath powders, pressing out excess air; place in envelope and seal closed with glue stick.

4. Tear irregular shape from sheer paper (or, trim edges of regular card stock with decorative paper edgers) and glue to center of envelope; glue assembled soap with card stock to center of sheer paper.

5. Tie ribbon around envelope in a bow; trim tails at an angle.

6. On computer or by hand, print "Fancy Bath Powders" on label; trim with scalloped paper edgers and affix to envelope. ✂

Jewel-Tone Mosaic Frame

Continued from page 47

2. In same manner, form two down-facing loops on each side of center loop, spacing all loops 1¼" apart.

3. Cut 20-gauge wire into four equal pieces. Form each into ½" coiled charm (Figs. 1–3).

4. From remaining 16-gauge wire form four jump rings, wrapping wire around widest part of pliers jaw. Attach charm to each downward loop using jump ring.

5. Tape photo to back of frame; hang frame in sunny window. ✂

Fig. 1

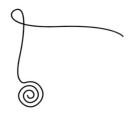

Fig. 2

Fig. 3

Glittering Love Soaps

Handcrafted soaps with your choice of fragrance make wonderful hostess gifts and surefire sellers at your craft bazaar.

Design by Katie Hacker

Materials

- 3 ounces clear glycerin melt-and-pour soap*
- 2¼"-tall letter molds to spell "LOVE"
- 2 pinches lilac soap coloring powder*
- ¼ teaspoon iridescent glitter*
- 2 drops fragrance*
- Microwave-safe glass measuring cup
- Craft stick

Soap, glitter, coloring powder and fragrance from Life of the Party.

Instructions

1. Microwave soap in measuring cup on HIGH for 40 seconds; stir with craft stick, then heat for 10-second intervals until melted.

2. Pour in glitter, fragrance and coloring powder, stirring thoroughly with craft stick.

3. Let cool until cup is warm—not hot—to the touch. Pour soap into molds; let cool 10–30 minutes. Using gentle thumb pressure, remove soap from molds. ✄

Bridal Shower Parasol

Here's the perfect decoration for a friend's bridal shower. You can make it extra-special by using remnants from her wedding gown to trim the parasol.

Design by Nazanin S. Fard

Materials

- 100-percent silk parasol*
- 4 yards scalloped lace edging
- 7½ yards ⅜"-wide white ribbon with printed pink flowers*
- 3 yards 2⅝"-wide gold-edge sheer ivory wire-edge nylon ribbon*
- 7 yards ⅞"-wide shaded pink polyester ombre ribbon*
- 42 medium green leaves*
- 16 pearl sprays
- Sewing needle and white thread
- Fabric glue*

*Arty's parasol, Garden Party pink #1511 ribbon and Virginia #16 polyester ombre ribbon from C.M. Offray, MW crystal #40 nylon ribbon and Neva Wilt leaves from Lion Ribbon Co., and Fabri-Tac adhesive from Beacon.

Gathered Roses

1. Pull out both wires of wire-edged ribbon ½" at one end; twist together.

2. At the other end, gather ribbon along one edge only, pushing toward twisted end.

3. Roll ribbon around gathered edge and secure with a few stitches; trim excess ribbon and wire.

Folded Roses

Note: *Refer to Figs. 1–4.*

1. Fold down right end of ribbon. Fold ribbon across once and roll five times to form center.

2. Fold back all the ribbon on left; tilt center and roll across fold. Stitch bottom edge of rose as you go. Repeat this step until all ribbon is used.

3. Secure with a few stitches. Trim excess ribbon and thread.

Instructions

1. Glue lace to edge of parasol. Glue three leaves at end of each spoke and two in between.

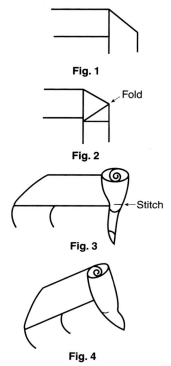

Fig. 1

Fig. 2 — Fold

Fig. 3 — Stitch

Fig. 4

2. Glue pearl spray at each leaf cluster.

3. Cut eight 20" pieces ⅜"-wide printed ribbon; tie each in a bow. Glue one at tip of each spoke.

4. Tie remaining printed ribbon into a bow with six folds; glue near top of parasol.

5. Cut eight 10" pieces sheer ivory nylon ribbon; make gathered rose from each and glue one over base of leaves at spoke tips.

6. With remaining ivory nylon ribbon, fashion large gathered rose; glue on top of bow at tip of parasol. Glue two leaves under it.

7. Cut 24 (10") pieces pink ombre ribbon; make folded rose from each. Glue two on either side of sheer ivory ribbon rose at each spoke tip and one to each leaf cluster between spokes. ✄

Summer
Sparkles!

Bright colors, golden rays of sunshine and oodles of crafting odds and ends make for a delightfully fun crafting combination! Fill your summer days with creating dozens of attractive home accents and gifts, and make your craft booth the most popular one at the show!

Ideas Everywhere!

Many of our best crafting ideas come from the wonderful craft and sewing magazines that we read each month. While you might not think of them as "scraps," a stash of magazines can reach overwhelming proportions when they start stacking up.

I found some wonderful ideas for using those magazines while surfing the Web. I've combined the best tips to give you some great ideas for using this resource to its fullest.

When you can't save one more magazine because your stacks are starting to resemble the Great Pyramids of Egypt, take some time and sort them. First, browse through each one and decide if you like one or two projects or if the whole magazine is worth saving. Rip out the projects you like and place them in a pile. Start a separate pile for complete magazines.

Place the ripped-out pages into files. Have a file for each type of craft project—one for sewing, one for glue crafts, one for dolls, etc. You can also place pages in page protectors; just slide pages for one project into each protector and file the protectors in binders.

Sometimes all you really need is an illustration or photo to serve as inspiration. Make a creative journal of photos for future motivation. Creative journals are also great for jotting down ideas and future project plans. Then, when you hit an artistic brick wall, just open your journals for a creative breakthrough.

Organize all of your magazines. Inside, write the date you organized the magazines. If six months or a year passes and you haven't used or referred to the magazines, it might be time to donate them to a school, senior center or community organization. ✂

Additional Tips & Ideas for Magazines

- Cut out and decoupage attractive images.
- Use single pages to protect your table or work space.
- Make paper beads with the slick pages.
- Substitute the paper for origami paper.
- Make envelopes.
- Use as gift wrap for a crafty friend.
- Use slick pages as paint palettes.

- Crimp up sides and use as a tray to catch stray beads, glitter or embossing powder.
- Use to press and dry flowers and leaves.
- Use for tea-bag folding.
- Cut into strips for weaving place mats.
- Use as backgrounds for greeting cards and rubber-stamping.

Daisies & Denim Scrapbook

*Ready-made appliqués and faux gemstones transform a three-ring binder
into a fun and sassy album for photos and other memorabilia.*

Design by Katie Hacker

Materials

- 10½" x 11" three-ring binder
- 6¾" x 8¾" white photo mat with opening for 4" x 6" photo
- 2 (10" x 10½") pieces poster board
- Daisy appliqués*: 3 (2½") blue, 3 (2") green
- Green acrylic rhinestones*: 22 (5mm), 3 (7mm)
- 21 green seed beads
- Beading needle and green thread
- Ribbon: 10" ⅝"-wide gold mesh, 10" 1⅜"-wide blue
- 2½ yards denim fabric
- 4" x 6" photo
- Spray adhesive
- Craft glue
- Acid-free tape
- Iron

Decorative Details appliqués and rhinestones from Hirschberg Schutz & Co.

Instructions

1. Iron fabric. Lay right side down; arrange binder and poster board pieces on fabric. Cut around binder leaving 1" allowance on all sides; cut around poster board leaving ½" allowance.

2. Spray adhesive onto outside of binder; lay it, open, on wrong side of fabric. *Miter corners:* Spread craft glue along inner edges of binder; fold fabric over edges smoothly and press into glue. At metal binder fixture, fold fabric over to create hem and slide under metal spine.

3. Spray adhesive onto poster board; lay on wrong side of fabric pieces. *Miter corners:* Make straight cut at one side of corner and cut other side at 45-degree angle.

Spread glue along edges of poster board; fold over straight-cut edges of fabric first, then angle-cut edges. Set aside.

4. Glue 7mm rhinestone in center of each blue daisy. Glue appliqués and rhinestones to photo mat. Tape photo to back of mat.

5. Using beading needle and green thread, sew seven seed beads in center of each daisy.

6. Glue gold ribbon down center of blue ribbon; let dry. Cut ribbon in half. Glue half to back of mat, one centered a top and one at bottom. Glue mat to front of album. Wrap ribbon inside album; glue down ends.

7. Glue covered poster board (step 3) inside each cover. ✄

Bee Nice

For Valentine's Day or any day, this little guy offers invaluable advice!

Design by Ginny Baker

Materials

- Polymer clay*: black, white, sunflower yellow, raspberry, Pacific blue, lavender, Indian red
- Heart cookie cutters: 1" and 1½"
- Black ball-head pins: 2 (1⁄16"), 2 (1½")
- ⅜" heart cutter*
- Needle tool
- Toothpick
- Acrylic paints: white, yellow, black (optional)
- Small paintbrush
- Black gel pen
- Wire cutters
- Rolling pin or acrylic brayer
- Baking sheet
- Plain white paper
- Ruler or circle template
- Oven

Fimo clay from Amaco; Kemper heart cutter.

Project Notes

Clean hands well when changing colors of clay; baby wipes work well. Do not use a rolling pin that has been used with polymer clay for food preparation.

Instructions

1. *Body:* Roll 1¼" ball black clay into rounded cone for body. Roll three ½" black balls and three ½" yellow balls into ropes; flatten slightly. Wrap around body, alternating colors and trimming as necessary with seams in back.

2. *Legs:* Roll two 1⅛" balls black clay into tapered logs; indent larger ends with thumb to form feet. Attach tapered ends to sides of body. Use heart cutter to indent hearts in feet (or use needle tool to draw hearts in feet).

3. *Arms:* Roll two 1" balls black clay into tapered logs; round off larger ends and flatten slightly to form hands. Attach tapered ends to top of body.

4. *Head:* Break toothpick in half; insert one half, pointed end up into top of body. Roll 1" ball black clay into egg shape; press larger end onto end of toothpick. Flatten ⅜" ball yellow into thin oval with slightly tapered ends; press onto face. Cut heads from 1⁄16" pins; press

into face for eyes. Use needle tool to make lash lines and eyebrows. Roll ¼" ball red clay into oval; press under eyes for nose. Use needle tool to poke hole for mouth.

5. *Wings:* Cut two 1½" hearts from ⅛"-thick white clay. Make check pattern with needle tool. Roll two tiny balls each of blue, raspberry and lavender clay for buttons; press onto wings, indenting slightly with head of pin and using needle tool to poke holes. Attach wings to body.

6. *Stinger:* Roll ¼" ball black clay into a rope; twist and attach to back of body.

7. *Bow tie:* Shape two ¼" balls blue clay into teardrops. Indent tops with needle tool to form hearts; press onto neck. Roll small ball blue; press onto center of bow. Use needle tool to indent center and add lines to bow.

8. *Heart:* Cut 1" heart from ³⁄16"-thick raspberry clay; place in bee's hands.

9. *Antennae:* Cut 1½" pins in half; insert in head.

10. Line baking sheet with white paper. Place bee on paper and bake in preheated 265-degree oven for 45 minutes; let cool completely.

11. Using toothpick dipped in white and yellow paints, add dip-dot flowers; dot white highlights onto eyes. Use gel pen to write "Bee Nice" on heart. Paint antennae stems black, if desired. ✄

Sculpted Spring Butterfly

Sculpt this friendly garden visitor to dress up a windowsill or whatnot shelf!

Design by Ginny Baker

Materials

- Polymer clay*: pastel mint green, pastel sky blue, pastel raspberry pink, white, sunflower yellow, raspberry, lavender, violet
- 3" butterfly cookie cutter
- 2 black 1‌1⁄16" ball-head pins
- 2" yellow craft wire
- Heart cutters* (optional): 3⁄8", 3⁄16"
- Teardrop cutters* (optional): 1", 1⁄2"
- Needle tool
- Toothpick
- Small paintbrush
- White acrylic paint
- Pink chalk
- Wire cutters
- Rolling pin or acrylic brayer
- Baking sheet
- Plain white paper
- Ruler or circle template
- Oven

Fimo clay from Amaco; Kemper heart and teardrop cutters.

Project Notes

Clean hands well when changing colors of clay; baby wipes work well. Do not use a rolling pin that has been used with polymer clay for food preparation.

Instructions

1. *Body:* Roll 1½" ball mint clay into rounded cone for body. Use needle tool to impress lines around body.

2. *Legs:* Roll two 1⅛" balls mint clay into tapered logs; indent larger ends with thumb to form feet. Attach tapered ends to sides of body.

3. *Arms:* Roll two 1" balls mint clay into tapered logs; round off larger ends and flatten slightly to form

hands. Attach tapered ends to top of body.

4. *Head:* Break toothpick in half; insert one half, pointed end up into top of body. Roll 1" ball mint clay into egg shape; press larger end onto end of toothpick. Cut heads from pins; press into face for eyes. Use needle tool to make lash lines. Roll 3⁄16" ball pastel raspberry clay into oval; press under eyes for nose. Use needle tool to draw smile. Rub paintbrush across chalk; blush cheeks.

5. *Wings:* Flatten 3" ball lavender 1⁄8" thick; cut butterfly with cookie cutter. Cut four 1" teardrops from 1⁄16"-thick pastel raspberry (or form teardrops from 3⁄8" balls pastel raspberry); cut four 1⁄2" teardrops from 1⁄16"-thick pastel sky blue (or form teardrops from 1⁄4" balls sky blue); press teardrops onto wings.

6. From 1⁄16"-thick raspberry, cut 14 (3⁄16") hearts (or, form 1⁄8" balls raspberry into teardrops, flatten slightly and indent tops with needle tool to form hearts). Press hearts onto tops of wings; poke holes in centers with needle tool. Roll 12 tiny balls raspberry; press onto bottoms of wings. Gently press wings in place.

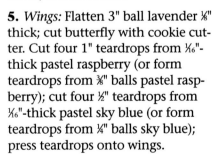

7. Cut two 3⁄8" hearts from pastel raspberry (or, form 1⁄4" balls pastel raspberry into teardrops, flatten

slightly and indent tops with needle tool); attach to centers of feet. Cut 3⁄16" heart from pale raspberry; attach to chest.

8. *Bow tie:* Cut two 3⁄8" hearts from 1⁄16"-thick violet clay (or, shape two 1⁄4" balls into teardrops and indent tops with needle tool); press onto neck. Press small ball violet onto center of bow. Use needle tool to indent center and add lines to bow.

9. *Flower:* Slightly flatten 3⁄8" ball yellow for center. Flatten six 1⁄4" balls white for petals; press around center. Press flower onto hands.

10. *Antennae:* Cut wire in half; curl one end of each and insert in head.

11. Line baking sheet with white paper. Place butterfly on paper and bake in preheated 265-degree oven for 45 minutes; let cool completely.

12. Using toothpick dipped in white, dot highlights onto eyes. ✂

Pink Roses Bottle

It's foolproof! This decorated decanter is the perfect container for a gift of lotion, bath salts, even flavored vinegars!

Design by Betsy H. Edwards

Materials

- Clear glass bottle
- Surface conditioner*
- Enamel paints*: apple candy green, desert blush pink, fuchsia
- Paintbrushes: #5 round, #0 liner

PermEnamel surface conditioner and paints from Delta.

Instructions

1. Wash and rinse bottle; dry.

2. Apply surface conditioner to outside of bottle.

3. Use #5 round brush to paint pink circles randomly on bottle. When dry, add a second coat.

4. Paint green leaf next to each circle, varying positions of leaves.

5. Load liner with fuchsia; paint spiral on each pink circle.

6. Rinse liner; load with green. Paint squiggly line around neck of bottle and paint rim around mouth.

7. Add a touch of fuchsia to green; use this darker green to add vein down center of each leaf and shade squiggly line around neck. ✄

Sponge-Painted Bottle

The warm hues of precious turquoise, gold and copper transform a simple glass bottle into a beautiful work of art. Only you will know how easy it was to make!

Design by Betsy H. Edwards

Materials

- Clear glass bottle with cork stopper
- Surface conditioner*
- Enamel paints*: azure blue, beyond turquoise, gold
- Sponge
- 24-gauge copper wire: 12" and 3 (10") pieces
- 6mm glass beads: turquoise, amber
- Sponge
- Natural silk sponge
- Wire cutters (optional)
- Knitting needle

PermEnamel surface conditioner and paints from Delta.

Instructions

1. Wash and rinse bottle; dry.

2. Apply surface conditioner to outside of bottle.

3. Dampen sponge; squeeze out excess water. Dip in puddle of azure blue; pounce on palette or paper towel to remove about half of paint. Pounce color on bottom 1½" of bottle and on shoulders, mouth and neck. Reload sponge as needed, though solid coverage is not necessary. Apply paint to cork in same manner.

4. Pounce sponge on paper towel until most of azure blue is removed. Dip sponge into puddle of turquoise; pounce to remove some paint, then pounce on bottle over azure blue, allowing some of darker color to show through. Sponge cork as well.

5. Pounce sponge on paper towels to remove as much paint as possible. Dip into puddle of gold and pounce on palette; lightly pounce over blue paint on bottle and cork. Let paints cure for at least 24 hours.

6. Put cork stopper in bottle. Hold 10" pieces of wire together; fold in half and wrap around cork near mouth of bottle. Insert six wire ends through loop formed by folding wire; pull until wire is tight. Twist cut ends of wire together at least eight times. Wrap wire around cork and tuck ends under wrapped wire.

7. Wrap 12" wire around neck of bottle and twist together three or four times. Thread turquoise bead, then amber bead onto wires; twist together two or three times. Wrap each wire end individually around knitting needle to curl. ✂

Olive Oil Bottle

Oils infused with herbs and seasonings make wonderful gifts!
Present your favorite recipe in this painted bottle.

Design by Betsy H. Edwards

Materials

- Empty oil bottle
- Surface conditioner*
- Enamel paints*: chocolate, hunter green, sea foam green, ultra black, ultra white
- Paintbrushes: #5 round, 10/0 liner
- Tracing paper
- Gray graphite paper
- 8 (9") pieces 20-gauge copper wire
- Needle-nose pliers

PermEnamel surface conditioner and paints from Delta.

Instructions

1. Wash bottle, removing labels and glue; rinse and dry.

2. Apply surface conditioner to outside.

3. Trace pattern onto tracing paper; tape onto bottle. Slip graphite paper under pattern graphite side down; trace over pattern lines. Remove pattern and lift off graphite paper.

4. Using liner, paint stem chocolate.

5. Load round brush with hunter green; tip into sea foam. Paint leaves and wavy line around shoulder of bottle.

6. Load round brush with hunter green; paint 1" strip around neck of bottle; let dry. Apply second coat. Using liner and hunter, paint "OLIVE OIL" on bottle.

7. Paint olives black; let dry; apply second coat; let dry. Dip brush into white; wipe most of paint off onto paper towel. Using nearly dry brush, dry-brush highlights on olives where indicated by short lines.

8. Hold wires together; fold in half and wrap around bottleneck. Using pliers, twist wires several times and curl cut ends. ✂

Olive Oil Bottle
Do not transfer short diagonal lines; these indicate areas to be dry-brushed

Summertime Soaps

By using this simple technique, you can create soaps to match virtually any bathroom decor!

Design by Samantha McNesby

Materials

- Bar white soap
- Paper napkins with ivy and ladybug motifs*
- Acrylic craft paints*: holly green, bright green
- Candle- and soap-painting medium*
- Satin-finish acrylic sealer
- ½" flat paintbrush
- Small, sharp scissors
- Small amount block paraffin (optional)
- Coffee can or double-boiler (optional)
- Disposable or foam brush (optional)

Samples were completed using Napkin Décor napkins N1 and N3, Candle and Soap Medium and Americana acrylic paints, all from DecoArt.

Ivy Soap

1. Blend candle- and soap-painting medium in holly green paint; paint stripes around sides with mixture; let dry.

2. Cut motif(s) from ivy napkin; arrange on top of soap. Remove cutouts.

3. Coat top and sides of soap with acrylic sealer. While still wet, lay cutouts on top of soap. Carefully coat cutouts with more sealer; let dry. Add one more coat sealer to top of soap; let dry.

Soaps completed to this point are for decorative use only. For more permanent, usable soaps, continue with step 4.

4. Carefully melt paraffin according to manufacturer's directions in old coffee can or other container. Apply a coat of melted paraffin to top of soap with disposable brush. Let cool and wait for 24 hours before using soap. Image will last the life of the soap.

Ladybug Soap

Repeat steps for ivy soap, substituting ladybug napkin and painting bright green stripes on sides. ✄

Painted Button Jar

Indispensable on the bureau or in the dressing room, this handy holder for stray buttons and pins is easy to make from a recycled jar.

Design by Betsy H. Edwards

Materials

- Small glass jar with lid*
- Acrylic enamel paints*: citrus yellow, fire red, emperor blue, true green, ultra white, ultra black
- Surface conditioner*
- Sponge
- Paintbrushes: 10/0 liner, #3 round
- 1" sponge brush (optional)

Sample was made using 4-ounce minced garlic jar; Ceramcoat PermEnamel paints and surface conditioner from Delta.

Instructions

1. Wash and dry jar and lid, removing label and glue.

2. Apply surface conditioner to jar and lid.

3. Wet sponge; squeeze out excess moisture. Dip sponge in puddle of white paint; pounce excess off onto paper towel. Pounce paint all over jar; apply two or three coats, allowing paint to dry between each.

Optional: Instead of sponge, apply paint with foam brush.

4. Using same method, paint lid blue.

5. Using #3 round brush, paint buttons of various sizes and colors on jar. Using liner, add "BUTTONS" in red and blue, and "PINS" in green.

6. Using liner and black, add simple drawings of needles and pins as desired; add threads, stitching lines, etc., with liner and desired color(s). ✄

String-of-Buttons Bracelet

To make a bracelet for an average adult wrist, you'll need 15" round elastic cord and 30–40 shank buttons. (Adjust the amount of materials as needed for wrists of different sizes; measure the wrist and use double that length of elastic cord.)

Thread buttons on elastic cord until you have approximately 12" of buttons with 3" of cording at the end.

Securely knot ends of cord together to form a solid circle of buttons. I recommend adding a drop of glue to the knot if you're making the bracelet for a child or teenager.

Double-wrap the button cluster around your wrist.

Make a set of matching earrings by simply gluing two matching buttons to post earring jewelry findings with jewelry glue. ✄

Buttoned-Up Topiary

Buttons … buttons … everyone has buttons! Buttons star on this whimsical topiary, beautiful for boudoir, sewing room or craft corner!

Design by Paula Bales

Materials

- Acrylic paints*: woodland green, valentine pink
- #12 shader paintbrush
- Crackle medium*
- 3"-diameter x 4"-tall terra-cotta flowerpot
- Plastic foam balls*: 2", 2½", 3"
- 14" ¼"-diameter dowel
- Craft cement*
- Low-temperature glue gun
- Tacky craft glue
- 1½" ribbon bow
- Assorted ½"–¾" green buttons
- ⅜" pink buttons
- Dried Spanish moss

Apple Barrel paints and crackle medium from Plaid; STYROFOAM plastic foam balls from Dow; E-6000 Adhesive from Eclectic.

Instructions

1. Paint dowel green; let dry.

2. Poke dowel through 3" plastic foam ball and glue; glue 2½" ball to top.

3. Glue on green buttons to cover balls; glue pink buttons atop green buttons. Glue Spanish moss and bow to top of 3" ball.

4. Paint pot green; let dry. Paint with crackle medium; let dry. Paint with pink; let dry.

5. Glue six ¾" dark green buttons around top of pot.

6. Push 2" foam ball inside pot; poke and glue end of dowel down into foam. Glue Spanish moss across top of pot to conceal foam. ✄

15 Fun Uses for Buttons

- Bingo markers
- Mobiles
- Button dolls
- Stamping textures
- Friendship bracelets
- Weights for outdoor picnic tablecloths
- Earrings
- Necklaces

- Brooches and pins
- Pieces for checkers game
- Centers for appliqué flowers
- Border for message or memo boards
- Eyes for dolls or stuffed animals
- Wind chimes
- Tack covers

Fruit Jar Lamp

Brighten a dark corner with this colorful, sponge-stamped lamp made from a recycled jar!
Using the same basic techniques, you can create lamps for any look!

Design by Doxie Keller

Materials

- 1-quart fruit jar
- Lamp kit*
- 8" paper or fabric lamp shade
- Acrylic enamel paints*: buttermilk, lemon yellow, cadmium yellow, burgundy, Christmas red, Christmas green, baby blue, true blue, yellow green, gloss black
- Paintbrushes: #2 script liner, spatter brush
- Miracle sponge*
- Fine-point permanent black marker

Lamp kit from Yesterday's Treasures, Ultra Gloss Acrylic Enamel paints from DecoArt, Miracle Sponge from The Color Wheel Co.

Instructions

1. Wash jar with soap and water; let dry. Cut 2" square from sponge; expand in water and squeeze out excess. Coat jar and lid using sponge dipped in buttermilk paint; let dry for 2–3 hours.

2. From sponge, cut ¾" square to stamp checkerboard pattern; cut also 1½" x 1½" and 2" x 4¼" hearts; 1⅛" x 1¾", ¾" x 1½", 1¼" x 3" and 2" x 2¼" rectangles. Expand shapes in water; squeeze out excess.

3. Apply true blue to ¾" square; stamp two rows of squares around bottom of jar checkerboard style, stamping three or four squares before reapplying paint.

4. Apply two complementary colors to each remaining sponge shape—burgundy with Christmas red, Christmas green with yellow green, true blue with baby blue, cadmium yellow with lemon yellow, etc. Stamp shapes over surface of jar, overlapping some. Let dry for 2 hours.

5. Outline stamped shapes with black marker.

6. Spatter lamp with black; spatter shade with all colors used on shapes. Let dry.

7. Assemble lamp according to manufacturer's instructions. ✂

Great Web Sites for Crafty Scrap Ideas

The Web sites listed are addresses for the home page of the site. Since Web sites are constantly being updated, sometimes a specific site address has been altered. However, from a home page you can click onto whatever project or medium you want.

General Crafting

www.freepatterns.com

www.craftygal.com

www.duncancrafts.com

www.fiskars.com

www.i-craft.com

Paper

www.allcrafts.net/cards.htm

www.seedsofknowledge.com

www.oldfashionedholidays.com

Polymer Clay & Beads

www.eebeads.com/Webzine/

www.frazz.com/howto.htm

www.chadiscrafts.com

Kids

www.craftbin.com/kidcrafts.htm

www.frugal-moms.com

www.hercraftideas.com

www.frugalliving.about.com/cs/craftshobbies

Needle Arts

www.freepatterns.com

www.joann.com

www.creativehomemaking.com

Gum Ball Beauties

Turn old mayo jars into a colorful treat jar and a clever accent lamp that will have friends and family looking twice!

Design by Delores F. Ruzicka

Materials

Each Project

- Quart jar with lid
- Acrylic enamel paints*: ultra white, lilac lace, Mediterranean blue, tangerine, silver, emperor blue, true green, fire red, eggplant, black, white frost
- Sea sponge
- Paintbrushes: ½" wash, size #11
- ½" circles cut from sponge
- Black fine-point permanent marker
- Craft cement*

Lamp

- 4" terra-cotta flowerpot
- Candelabra wiring kit

Treat Jar

- 9 (¾") wooden balls

*PermEnamel paints from Delta; Crafter's Pick Ultimate glue.

Lamp

1. Punch or cut ½" hole in center of jar lid. Glue lid to bottom of flowerpot, aligning holes, so jar can be screwed onto pot later; let dry.

2. Using ½" brush, paint flowerpot and lid red; add a second coat if needed. Let dry.

3. Using #1 brush, paint coin slot, handle and spout on front of flowerpot with black and silver paints; paint "Gum Balls 5¢" with ultra white.

4. Dip sea sponge in white frost and pounce all over surface of jar; let dry.

5. Using a separate circle for each color, dip sponge circles into paints and stamp gum balls onto jar; let dry.

6. Outline gum balls with marker.

7. Wire flowerpot with candelabra kit; screw jar onto flowerpot.

Treat Jar

1. Using ½" brush, paint lid red; add a second coat if needed. Let dry.

2. Paint wooden balls an assortment of colors; let dry, then glue in a pile on top of lid.

3. Repeat steps 4–6 as for lamp.

4. Using #1 brush, paint "Candy" on jar with red. ✂

Uses for Felt Scraps

- Absorbers, cushions or spacers
- Air fresheners
- Banners and boards
- Nonstick and scratch protectors
- Brushes and sponges
- Liners for boxes and shadow box frames
- Polishing and burnishing

- Erasers for chalk and memo boards
- Doll hair
- Stuffing
- Stamp pads
- Finger puppets
- Thimbles
- Doll clothes
- Kids' jewelry

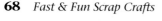

Beaded Bracelet Candle

How pretty this is—and what a great showcase for one-of-a-kind beads and charms!
Change the look instantly with a different "bracelet."

Design by Katie Hacker

Materials

- ¾ cup clear gel wax*
- 3" x 2¾" clear glass ivy bowl
- 4¾" wick with wick clip*
- Purple candle dye*
- ¼ teaspoon fine iridescent glitter
- Assorted 6mm–8mm glass beads
- 8" elastic cord
- Craft sticks
- Transparent tape
- Pliers
- Pan with pour spout
- Candy thermometer
- Kitchen stove

Candle supplies from Yaley.

Project Note

Extinguish candle before it burns within ½" of bottom.

Instructions

1. String wick in clip; crimp clip with pliers.

2. Break gel wax into 1"–2" pieces. Place in pan and melt, following manufacturer's instructions, stirring frequently with craft stick and monitoring temperature with thermometer. Add dye in small shavings until desired color is reached.

3. Dip wick clip in melted wax; position in center bottom of bowl and press in place with stick. Lay craft stick across top of jar and wrap top of wick around it to hold it straight. Secure with tape.

4. Pour wax into bowl. Let cool undisturbed.

5. Trim wick to ¼".

6. String beads onto elastic; knot ends together. Slip bracelet over candle holder. ✂

Wire & Marbles Candle Plate

Combine crafting leftovers to create an eye-catching accent in next to no time!

Design by Katie Hacker

Materials

- Plastic coated wire*: 42" 24-gauge icy blue "fizzy," 48" 18-gauge and 36" 24-gauge icy silver
- 18 iridescent turquoise E beads*
- Flat glass marbles: 19 turquoise, 8 clear
- 7½"-diameter clear glass candle plate
- 2½" x 6" white pillar candle
- Clear silicone adhesive
- Wire cutters
- Round-nose and flat-nose pliers

Fun Wire from Toner Plastics; glass beads from Hands of the Hills.

Instructions

1. Glue marbles around edge of plate within 1¾" of rim; let dry.

2. Form loop in end of 18-gauge silver wire with round-nose pliers. Grasp loop with flat-nose pliers and turn it to form four-turn coil at end of wire. Wrap wire around marbles on plate, using pencil to make coils and round-nose pliers to make freeform patterns as you work. Form two-turn coil at other end; connect ends.

3. With blue and silver 24-gauge wires, make free-form patterns around marbles and 18-gauge silver wire on plate. Add E beads in six groups of three beads each, spacing evenly along 24-gauge silver wire. ✄

Superstar T-Shirt

Dress up a plain T-shirt with glittering stars using stencils and fabric paints.

Design by Phyllis Sandford

Materials

- Red short-sleeved T-shirt
- String-of-stars stencil*
- Fabric colors*: robin blue, starlight white, wild berry
- Sparkling gold (clear) glittering fabric color*
- Multicolored liquid confetti*
- Stencil-sponge holder*
- Small pieces stencil sponge
- Repositionable stencil adhesive spray*
- Palette paper
- Shirt-painting board

Stencil Magic stencil #95-113-0012, Starlite Dye Shimmering and Glitter fabric colors, Christmas Dazzlers liquid confetti, Stencil Buddy sponge holder and stencil adhesive, all from Delta.

Project Note

Use a clean piece of sponge for each color paint. Pounce excess color onto palette paper before stenciling shirt.

Instructions

1. Wash and dry shirt without using fabric softener. Place shirt-painting board inside shirt.

2. Spray back of star stencil with adhesive spray; position on shirt with large star at center front. Stencil large star with blue; stencil remaining stars with blue, white and gold. Stencil ribbon with berry.

3. Brush liquid confetti over white stars, selecting stars from confetti.

4. Let paint dry according to manufacturer's instructions before wearing or laundering. ✂

Patriotic Pride T-Shirt

Perfect for those summertime cookouts and fireworks celebrations, this blue T-shirt boasts a bold flag motif.

Design by Mary Ayers

Materials

- Blue T-shirt
- Cotton fabrics: ¼ yard horizontal red print, ⅛ yard white print or solid
- 3 (¾"-wide) flat buttons
- Iron-on adhesive*
- Dark red embroidery floss
- Embroidery needle
- Iron

HeatnBond Ultra Hold from Therm O Web.

Instructions

1. Wash and dry T-shirt and fabrics without using fabric softener. Iron as needed.

2. Following manufacturer's instructions, fuse adhesive to backs of fabrics. Referring to patterns, cut three stars from white; cut stripes section from red, making sure stripes run horizontally.

3. Peel backing from fabrics; fuse star to each sleeve, and star and stripes to front.

4. Using 3 strands red floss, sew button in center of each star. Embroider buttonhole stitch around each star and around stripes section. ✂

Patterns continued on page 75

Beaded Doll Necklace

Your collection of crafting leftovers probably includes most all the beads you'll need for this charming necklace.

Design by Barbara Matthiessen

Materials

- Round wooden beads*: 2 (6mm) black, 4 (6mm) red, 4 (6mm) blue, 6 (6mm) natural, 4 (10mm) natural, 2 (12mm) natural, 6 (12mm) blue, 4 (12mm) red, 6 (14mm) natural
- 2 (10mm) red barrel wooden beads*
- 2 (1" x ⅛") wooden heart cutouts*
- Acrylic paints*: red apple, too blue, white, pastel pink
- Paintbrushes and tools: shader, liner brush, rake
- Fabric glue
- 28" red satin rattail cord
- 6-strand embroidery floss: red, blue
- 24" nylon fishing line or clear monofilament
- Black fine-point permanent marker
- Craft drill with ½" bit

FibreCraft beads; cutouts from Lara's Crafts; Apple Barrel acrylic paints from Plaid.

Instructions

1. Drill hole down edges of each heart from tip to center point where lobes meet.

2. Paint hearts red. Thin white paint slightly with water; dip rake in mixture and sweep across hearts diagonally; repeat, sweeping in the opposite direction. Using liner, paint a couple of blue diagonal lines in each direction across heart.

3. *Doll heads:* Dab two pink dots in center of two 12mm natural beads for cheeks; dot eyes with black marker.

4. *Hair:* Cut short lengths of red floss; glue to heads for bangs. Cut 2" floss for girl's hair; glue across top of head. Glue 1" strands across top of boy's head. When dry, trim as needed.

5. *Boy doll's body:* Cut 12" fishing line. Thread line through barrel bead (Fig. 1), then down into 12mm blue bead. Thread blue 6mm bead and black 6mm bead onto each line end. Bring line out of last bead, then back up through 6mm bead above it and 12mm blue bead. Thread lines back through barrel bead, tighten and knot off. Slide knot inside barrel bead.

6. *Girl doll's body:* Cut 12" fishing line. Thread line through

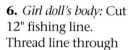
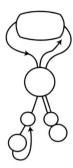

Fig. 1

Patriotic Pride T-Shirt

Continued from page 73

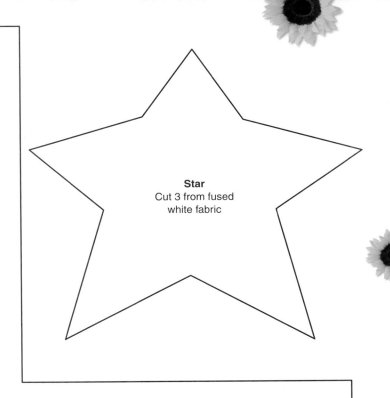

Star
Cut 3 from fused
white fabric

Stripes
Cut 1 from fused red-and-white
print fabric

Beaded Doll Necklace

barrel bead (Fig. 1), then down into one 12mm blue bead. Thread natural 6mm bead, then blue 6mm bead onto each line end. Bring line out of last bead, then back up through 6mm bead above it and 12mm blue bead. Thread lines back through barrel bead, tighten and knot off. Slide knot inside barrel bead.

7. Thread beads onto red cord in order: 14mm natural, 12mm red, 10mm natural, 14mm natural, 12mm blue, heart, 12mm blue, 14mm natural, 10mm natural, 12mm red, 6mm natural, 6mm red, barrel bead from doll's body, 6mm red, 6mm natural, 6mm natural, 6mm red, second barrel bead, 6mm red, 6mm natural, 12mm red, 10 mm natural, 14mm natural, 12mm

blue, heart, 12mm blue, 14mm natural, 10mm natural, 12mm red and 14mm natural.

8. Push beads together in center of cord. Tie overhand knots next to beads on ends. Adjust total length of cord, then tie ends together.

9. Glue doll heads atop correct barrel beads. Tie blue floss bows around dolls' necks. ✂

Birthday Balloons Set

Colorful balloons send happy greetings aloft with this collection featuring a T-shirt and headband for the birthday girl and a garland to hang on the door or wall.

Designs by Paula Bales

Materials

T-Shirt
- White T-shirt
- T-shirt painting board
- Acrylic paints*: white, cobalt blue, bright yellow, bright magenta, spring green, black
- Acrylic textile medium*
- Tip pen set*
- Small swirl sponge stamp*
- Paintbrushes: ⅜" angler, #1 round
- Straight pin

Headband
- Plastic headband
- Acrylic paints*: white, bright yellow, bright magenta, spring green
- Paintbrushes: #8 shader, #5/0 round
- 2 (12") pieces 18-gauge silver armature wire*
- Pure black marker*
- 2" x 24" x ⅛" basswood sheet*
- 2 yards ⅜"-wide yellow ribbon
- Hot-glue gun
- Wire cutters

Garland
- Acrylic paints*: white, cobalt blue, bright yellow, bright magenta, spring green, black
- ⅜" angler paintbrush
- Tip pen set*
- 50" 18-gauge silver armature wire*
- Pure black marker*
- Cardboard
- Wire cutters

Apple Barrel paints, textile medium, pen set, Fun to Paint sponge stamp and armature wire, all from Plaid; ZIG Memory System Millennium #MS08 writer from EK Success Ltd.; basswood from Midwest Products.

T-Shirt

1. Secure T-shirt on board. Enlarge pattern (page 78) 125 percent; referring to instructions for "Using Transfer & Graphite Paper" (General Instructions, page 174), transfer balloon outline to front of shirt.

2. Blend textile medium with blue, magenta, yellow and green paints. Paint one balloon with each color; let dry.

3. Trace lettering onto balloons. Paint lettering white with tip pen; outline balloons and add strings with black and tip pen.

4. Add magenta swirls with sponge; paint yellow slashes randomly on shirt. Using end of brush handle dipped in blue and head of straight pin dipped in green, dot shirt randomly.

5. Heat-set paint in hot dryer for at least 30 minutes.

Birthday Garland
Cut balloons from cardboard
Enlarge 150% before tracing

Birthday Balloons T-Shirt
Enlarge pattern 125% before
transferring onto T-shirt

Headband

1. Trace balloon outlines onto basswood; cut out. Paint balloons magenta and green; let dry.

2. Trace lettering onto balloons. Paint lettering white; add dots with head of straight pin dipped in yellow. Outline balloons, dots and lettering with black marker.

3. Wrap one end of each piece of wire around base of a balloon; wrap other ends around headband.

4. Glue one end of ribbon to end of headband; wrap headband with ribbon and glue other end.

Garland

1. Enlarge balloon patterns (page 76) 150 percent; trace onto cardboard

and cut out. Paint balloons blue, magenta, yellow and green; let dry.

2. Trace lettering onto balloons. Paint lettering white with tip pen; outline balloons with black marker.

3. Twist wire twice around base of each balloon, leaving 8" between balloons and 20" below last balloon. Curl wire between balloons around pencil. ✂

Birthday Balloons Headband
Cut balloons from basswood

Easy-to-Make Paper Beads

You'll need: scraps of paper, knitting needle, metal or bamboo skewers or toothpicks, scissors, ruler, paper glue, beading thread, dental floss or nylon thread. *Optional:* sealer (like glaze, varnish, or decoupage glue)

Instructions

1. Cut paper into strips about ½" wide and 12" long. Cut the strips into rectangles for tube-shaped beads or into long triangles for tapered beads.

2. Begin rolling a strip of paper

tightly around knitting needle (or skewer or toothpick). If you are making tapered beads, begin with the wide end. Hold the knitting needle firmly between your thumbs and index fingers, and with steady pressure, roll the paper around the knitting needle until you get to within 1"–2" of the end. Dab a bit of glue on the end and continue rolling it. Hold the end down until it sticks and then slide the bead off the knitting needle.

3. As you complete beads, set each aside to dry.

4. *Optional:* When all beads are complete, you may make the beads water resistant by coating them with sealer, brushing it on while the bead is on a skewer or toothpick so the bead hole will not be plugged with sealer. Remove the bead(s) from the skewers when dry.

5. Have fun experimenting with different sizes and shapes of beads, plus vary your assortment of paper scraps. You'll have plenty for making a pair of earrings, a bracelet or necklace. ✂

"You Lite Up My Life" T-Shirt

Colorful puffy paints give this T-shirt an added dimension of fun. Youngsters will love it!

Design by June Fiechter

Materials

- Child's light blue T-shirt
- Matte-finish puff paints*: yellow, pink, purple, blue, turquoise, green, orange, peach, spring green
- White iris glitter paint
- Fabric paints: blue, black
- ⅛" fabric paintbrush
- Iron

Jones Tones Matte Finish Puff Paint.

Instructions

1. Wash and dry shirt without using fabric softener. Enlarge pattern 125 percent; transfer pattern onto shirt as needed.

2. Paint large bug's wings turquoise. Paint bug pink; shade with purple; paint cheeks peach and squeeze on a pink heart for nose. Paint heart orange. Paint bottom of bug yellow; shade with orange. Brush light from bug around bottom with yellow; brush glitter on top of yellow.

3. Paint small bug body pink and wings blue.

4. Paint heart flower pink; shade with orange. Paint other flowers as desired using yellow, orange, blue, pink, purple and peach. Paint stems and leaves spring green; embellish with green.

5. Add lettering with blue.

6. Using black, add simple dot eyes to small bug; add antennae, eyebrows, eyes, mouth and legs to large bug.

7. Allow paints to dry. Puff with iron following manufacturer's instructions.

8. Using glitter paint, highlight flowers as desired and wings on small bugs; brush in large bug's flight path down to edge of shirt. ✂

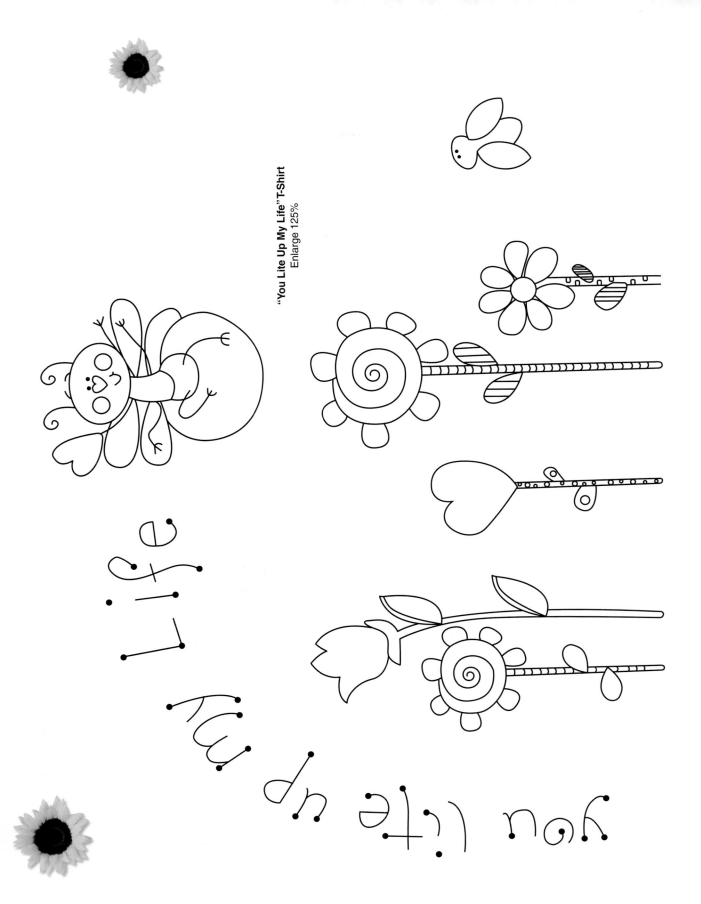

"You Lite Up My Life" T-Shirt
Enlarge 125%

Flowered & Jeweled Sunglasses

Sunglasses are great flea-market finds! Turn them into works of art with colorful paints and "jewels" left over from other projects!

Designs by Betsy H. Edwards

Materials

Flowered Sunglasses

- Black sunglasses of any size
- Rubbing alcohol
- Enamel craft paints*: ultra white, citrus yellow, fuchsia, light blue, tangerine, red red, apple candy green, hunter green
- Paintbrushes: #1 round, #10/0 liner
- Round wooden toothpick

Jeweled Sunglasses

- Sunglasses (see Project Note)
- Rubbing alcohol
- Faceted acrylic rhinestones: magenta 14mm heart, 2 green 12mm and 2 green 6mm marquises, 6 white 4mm rounds, 4 magenta 4mm rounds, 2 magenta 6mm teardrops
- Jewel glue*

Samples were made using Delta PermEnamel paints and Gem-Tac glue from Beacon.

Project Note

Child's metallic green sunglasses were used for sample jeweled sunglasses.

Flowered Sunglasses

1. Clean sunglasses frames with rubbing alcohol.

2. Paint flowers and leaves on frames as desired, adding dots with tip of paintbrush handle and/or toothpick dipped in paint.

3. Allow painted sunglasses to cure for several days before wearing.

Jeweled Sunglasses

1. Clean sunglasses frames with rubbing alcohol.

2. Glue gems to glasses frames.

3. Allow glue to set for 24 hours before wearing. ✂

Ribbon-Trimmed Memo Board

Adapt this design to use up your remnants of ribbon and trim that are too pretty to pitch!

Design by Katie Hacker

Materials

- 16" x 20" poster frame with cardboard backing
- 16" x 20" foam-core board
- 18" x 22" purple-and-white gingham fabric
- Ribbon: 1½ yards ⅝"-wide purple satin, 3 yards ⅜"-wide white satin picot-edge, 5¾ yards ⅝"-wide pink satin
- 4 (½") pink ribbon roses
- 22 clear 7mm acrylic rhinestones
- Sawtooth hanger
- White paint
- Clear acrylic sealer
- 1" foam brush
- Craft glue
- Spray adhesive
- Craft knife
- Double-sided adhesive tape

Instructions

1. Attach sawtooth hanger to top back of frame. Paint frame white; let dry. Apply a coat of sealer; let dry.

2. Cut two 17" and two 21" pieces pink ribbon; glue to sides of frame. Glue rhinestones on ribbons around frame.

3. Cut four 8" pieces white ribbon. Fold each into a bow shape and secure with double-sided tape; trim tails to 1½" and notch. Glue a bow to each corner; glue ribbon rose in center of each bow.

4. Lay fabric right side down. Spray foam-core board with adhesive and lay adhesive side down in center of fabric. Turn over; gently smooth fabric, pressing bubbles toward edges.

5. *Miter fabric corners:* Cut fabric at 45-degree angle. Fold excess fabric smoothly to back and glue with craft glue.

6. Lay pink ribbon diagonally across board 3¼" from lower left corner. Cut ribbon, leaving ends long enough to tape onto back of board. Attach another piece every 2¾" until there are seven pink ribbons running in same direction.

7. Using same method, attach white and purple ribbons in opposite direction, alternating colors and weaving them over and under pink ribbons.

8. Spray adhesive on back of foam board; attach to cardboard and place in frame. ✂

Silver Photo Plaque

Use a simple stamping technique to easily transform plaques of all sizes into elegant keepsakes and wonderful gifts!

Design by Joan Fee

Materials

- Stamp with opening in center for photo
- Wooden plaque with beveled edge slightly larger than stamp
- Silver spray paint
- White card stock
- Embossing ink pad
- Silver embossing powder
- Heat tool
- Deckle-edge paper edgers
- White paint pen
- Bead tape
- Silver micro beads
- Tray or box lid
- Photo tape
- Foam tape
- Photo to fit in stamp opening

Instructions

1. Spray-paint plaque silver.

2. Dab embossing pad onto stamp; immediately stamp card stock. Sprinkle stamped surface with silver embossing powder and, referring to manufacturer's instructions, heat to complete embossed effect.

3. When cool, trim around edges of design with deckle-edge paper edgers. Trim opening for photo from center.

4. Lay stamped card stock on front of plaque. Using white pen, draw designs in margins of plaque's surface to mimic stamped design. Remove card stock.

5. Apply bead tape along plaque's beveled edges. Remove protective film. Place plaque in tray; sprinkle beads over tape, pressing into place with fingers.

6. Using photo tape, tape picture behind opening in card stock. Position foam tape on back of card stock; position card stock with photo on plaque. ✄

"Hoppy" Birthday Journal

Gather your scrapbooking leftovers to make this special birthday keepsake.

Design by Marilyn Gossett

Materials

- Poster board
- White card stock
- Memory book papers: green-and-blue plaid, white-and-green stripe
- Green paper for filler
- Wooden cutouts*: large oval, 2 medium stars, 2 small stars, 2 small circles
- Acrylic paints*: light foliage green, white, black
- Acrylic varnish*
- ½" angular paintbrush
- Stylus or round toothpick
- 2 (5") pieces ¼" moss green satin ribbon
- Ultrafine-point black permanent marker
- Paper edgers: large and small scallops
- 24-gauge copper wire
- Wire cutters
- Glue stick

Woodsies cutouts from Forster; Ceramcoat paints and varnish from Delta.

"Hoppy" Birthday Journal

Project Notes

Refer to pattern. Let all paints, ink and varnish dry between coats.

Painting

1. Thin green paint with water to make a wash.

2. *Frog head:* Glue small circles (eyes) to top of oval. Paint with green wash.

3. *Face:* Paint bottom half of eyes white; dot black pupil onto each.

4. *Hands and feet:* Paint stars with green wash.

5. Apply white highlight dot to cheeks, hands and feet.

6. Add details with marker.

Journal

1. *Cut papers:* From poster board cut two 4" squares and one 3" square. From plaid paper cut two 5" squares and 4" x 8" rectangle. From striped paper cut 4" square and 4" x 3" rectangle (binding). From white card stock cut 4" square. From green filler paper cut four 3¾" x 7½" rectangles.

2. *Covers:* Center 4" square of poster board on wrong side of 5" plaid square. Miter corners and fold paper over edges of poster board;

glue. Repeat to make second cover.

3. *Front cover panel:* Repeat step 2 using 3" square of poster board and 4" striped square.

4. Glue front cover panel (step 3) right side up in center of white card stock. Trim card stock with small scalloped edgers leaving ¼" border.

5. *Sign:* Using large scalloped edgers, cut 2½" circle from white card stock; glue in center of 3½" circle cut from plaid paper. Trim plaid paper with small scalloped edgers, leaving ¼" border.

6. Glue sign in center of front

cover panel; glue panel in center of front cover. Add sentiment and outline with black marker.

7. *Legs:* Tie knot in center of one piece of ribbon. Glue one larger star to one end; glue other end inside bottom edge of front cover. Repeat for second leg.

8. Glue head and hands to top edge of front cover.

9. *Binding:* Fold 4" x 3" piece striped paper lengthwise into thirds, folding sides toward middle; glue.

10. Lay covers right side down and side by side, leaving ¼" gap between edges. Apply glue to inner edges of covers; lay binding strip over open seam, adhering to both covers. Smooth firmly; let glue dry.

11. Close journal, pressing binding so journal lies flat.

12. *Inner covers:* Glue 4" x 8" plaid paper inside journal covers to cover raw edges; smooth in place.

13. *Pages:* Fold green filler paper in half; insert between covers. Hold pages in place by wrapping wire around fold and binding and twisting to secure; trim, leaving 12" wire ends. Coil wire ends around skewer or similar object to spiral; bend end of each wire so it doesn't scratch. ✄

Lollipop Ornaments

These sweet trims look equally adorable hanging from a tree or gracing the packages beneath it.

Design by Mary Ayres

Materials
Each Ornament

- 2½" wooden craft disk*
- Craft stick*
- 10" 20-gauge gold wire
- 10" ¼"-wide white picot-edge satin ribbon
- Ultrafine glitter
- Acrylic paints*: white wash, plus royal fuchsia, pumpkin or bright green
- #8 natural bristle paintbrush
- Small sponge (optional)
- Swirl sponge stamp*
- Glue*
- Craft drill with ³⁄₃₂" bit
- Scrap wood
- Fine sandpaper

*Forster wooden products; Americana acrylic paints from DecoArt; Fun to Paint stamp #50125 from Plaid; Kids Choice Glue from Beacon.

Instructions

1. Place disk on scrap wood; drill two holes 2" apart near edge. Sand lightly. Paint disk white; let dry.

2. Dip brush or small sponge into puddle of pumpkin, green or fuchsia; dab onto sponge stamp. Press stamp onto center of disk's curved surface. Remove carefully; let dry.

3. Dilute a little glue with a little water. Dip brush or small sponge in mixture and dab onto sponge stamp. Press onto disk, avoiding areas painted in step 2. While still wet, sprinkle with glitter; shake off excess. Let dry.

4. Glue 1¼" of craft stick to back of disk, positioning holes at center top. Let dry.

5. Tie ribbon in bow around stick; trim ends.

6. Curl wire around pencil; slide off. Insert ends in holes and twist; shape wire into hanger. ✄

Ice-Cream Cone Place Cards

Here's a charming design that works equally well as a place card or a hanging ornament.

Design by Mary Ayres

Materials

Two Place Cards

- 2 (3" x 2") chalkboards with wooden frames and gold hangers
- 4 (1½") wooden teardrops*
- Acrylic paints*: white wash, mink tan, milk chocolate, baby pink, royal, fuchsia, orchid, lavender, baby blue, sapphire, mint julep green, bright green, white pearl, emperor's gold
- Paintbrushes: #6 round, #5 natural hair
- Mini-dot alphabet stencil*
- Extra-fine-tip opaque permanent writers*: white, gold
- Glue*
- Scrap of wire window screen
- Ultrafine glitter

Woodsies wooden teardrops from Forster; Americana acrylic paints from DecoArt; Plaid stencil #28036; ZIG Memory System writers from EK Success Ltd.; Kids Choice Glue from Beacon.

Instructions

1. Paint cone areas on teardrops tan; let dry. For texture, lay scrap of screen on painted cones; dry-brush milk chocolate through screen with dabbing motion (refer to directions for dry-brushing under "Painting Techniques" in the General Instructions, page 174).

2. Paint each ice-cream scoop a different color and dry-brush edges: pink with fuchsia dry-brushing, mint julep with bright green dry-brushing, orchid with lavender dry-brushing, and baby blue with sapphire dry-brushing. Let dry. Using brush handle dipped in white, dot upper right side of each ice-cream scoop; let dry.

3. Brush glue along edge of each scoop. While wet, sprinkle with glitter; shake off excess.

4. Paint chalkboard frames white wash; let dry, then paint with white pearl.

5. Draw "stitching line" around frame with gold writer. Stencil name in center of chalkboard with emperor's gold. Using white writer, draw "stitching line" around each letter.

6. Glue cones to frame. ✂

Sunflower Clock

Who would guess that a used CD hides behind the center of this sunny, lightweight clock?

Design by June Fiechter

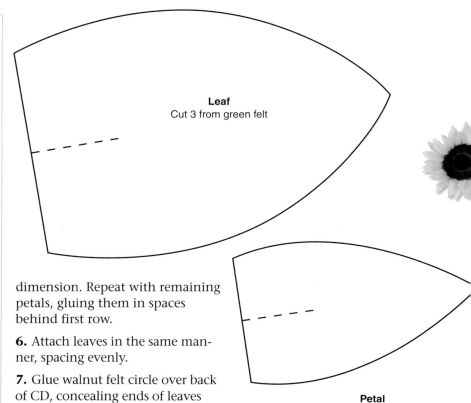

Leaf
Cut 3 from green felt

Petal
Cut 16 from butterscotch felt

Materials

- Used CD
- Clock mechanism*
- Embossed felt*: butterscotch, walnut, leaf green
- Matte 3D paints*: spearmint, cocoa, red red, basic black
- Paper glaze*
- 2 (¾") pieces black plastic-coated wire*
- Natural raffia
- Textile adhesive*
- Pinking shears
- Size 6 round fabric-painting brush
- Acrylic paints*: true apricot, true lime, true green, burnt umber

Clock mechanism from Walnut Hollow; Kunin felt; Tulip Matte 3D Paints, Aleene's Paper Glaze, Aleene's Platinum Bond Super Fabric textile adhesive and Aleene's Premium-Coat acrylic paints, all from Duncan; Artistic Wire.

Instructions

1. Using scissors, cut 16 petals from butterscotch felt and three leaves from green; snip petals and leaves along dashed lines. Using pinking shears, cut two 5½" circles from walnut felt.

2. Brush outer edges of petals with apricot paint; brush outer edges of leaves with lime; brush along snips and down leaf centers with green. Let dry.

3. Outline leaves and petals with broken line of cocoa 3D paint applied straight from bottle. Let dry.

4. Brush all felt pieces with two coats paper glaze; let dry.

5. Glue eight petals around CD, spacing evenly and folding slightly along centers to give petals

dimension. Repeat with remaining petals, gluing them in spaces behind first row.

6. Attach leaves in the same manner, spacing evenly.

7. Glue walnut felt circle over back of CD, concealing ends of leaves and petals.

Flowerpot Party Favor

*Turn kids on to the joys of crafting with this clever design! In just minutes,
transform plain-Jane flowerpots into dishes for delectable ice-cream "potting soil."*

Design by Shelia Sommers

Materials

Each Flowerpot

- Small terra-cotta flowerpot
- Acrylic paints*: white, periwinkle blue, Lisa pink, crocus yellow
- Paintbrushes: ⅜" glaze, #3 and #5 rounds
- Acrylic jewels: 4 or 5 gold stars, 4 or 5 small purple rounds
- Clear-drying glue

"Potting Soil"

- Colored plastic wrap
- Ice cream
- Crushed chocolate sandwich cookies
- Gummy worms

Ceramcoat paints from Delta.

Flowerpots

1. Wash each flowerpot in warm, soapy water. Rinse and allow to dry completely.

2. Paint base of pot white; let dry, then add second coat.

3. Paint wide blue stripes around pot with ⅜" brush; let dry. Using #5 round, paint narrow yellow stripes on white near blue stripes, and squiggly pink stripes on blue stripes near edge. Let dry.

4. Glue stars to rim of pot and purple jewels in centers of white stripes; let dry.

Assembling Favors

1. Line pot with plastic wrap.

2. Fill ⅛ full with softened ice cream; sprinkle with crushed cookies. Repeat layers to fill pot, ending with crushed cookies. Stuff a couple of gummy worms into ice cream; return to freezer until serving time.

3. When the party is over, send your guests home with a painted flowerpot that can be used to hold markers or pencils. ✄

Sunflower Clock

8. Cut small hole in center of walnut felt just large enough to fit stem of clock mechanism. Push mechanism from back to front; glue mechanism to CD.

9. Cut matching hole in second felt circle; glue to front of CD.

10. Mix a little black paint with water; dot onto center of walnut flower center.

11. Using red dimensional paint, form ladybugs on front of clock at 3, 6 and 9 o'clock positions; form a larger ladybug at 12 o'clock. Add heads and dots with black dimensional paint.

12. Coil end of wire pieces for antennae; push straight ends into head of large ladybug; let dry.

13. Tie lengths of raffia around center of clock mechanism. Complete clock assembly. ✄

Chenille-Trimmed Pillows

Arranged on a sofa or piled on a bed, this trio of colorful pillows begs to be hugged!

Designs by Fran Rohus

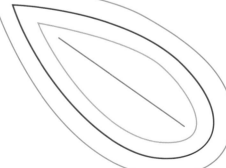

Materials

Daisy
- Cotton fabrics: ½ yard bright orange, ¼ yard bright yellow
- 1½ yards ¼" bright orange piping
- 3 (1") yellow buttons
- Chenille trim*: 70" blue moon, 60" grape soda, 50" limeade, 30" raspberry
- 14" pillow form

Swirl
- Cotton fabrics: ½ yard bright blue, ¼ yard bright green
- 1½ yards ¼" bright blue piping

- 3 (1") blue buttons
- Chenille trim*: 40" blueberry, 40" limeade
- 14" pillow form

Mini Geometric
- ½ yard purple cotton fabric
- 1 yard ¼" bright blue piping
- 3 (⅞") purple buttons

- Chenille trim*: 45" blueberry, 45" blue moon, 40" limeade, 20" grape soda
- 9" pillow form

Each Pillow
- Fusible interfacing
- Needle and matching threads
- Sewing machine (optional)
- Transfer or graphite paper
- Chenille cutting guide*
- Chenille brush*
- Spray bottle filled with water

Chenille By the Inch, Chenille Brush and Chenille Cutting Guide from Fabric Café.

Project Notes

Refer to patterns throughout; enlarge patterns as labeled before transferring to fabric. See instructions for "Using Transfer &

Graphite Paper" in the General Instructions, page 174. Use ½" seam allowances throughout.

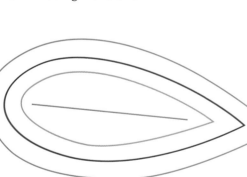

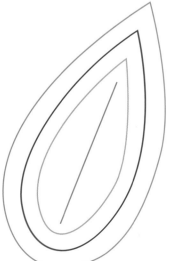

COLOR KEY
— Blue moon
— Grape soda
— Limeade
— Raspberry

Daisy Pillow
Enlarge pattern 200% before transferring

COLOR KEY
---- Blue moon
—— Grape soda
—— Limeade
—— Blueberry

Daisy Pillow

1. From orange fabric cut two 8" squares and one piece 15" x 11"; cut same pieces from yellow fabric. Cut two strips 15" x 2" from fusible interfacing.

2. Right sides facing, sew 8" blocks together in a four-square block for pillow front, alternating colors.

3. Transfer design to pillow front.

4. Remove tear-away backing from chenille trim; cut into long strips using cutting guide.

5. Sew strips to pillow front, back-tacking at beginning and end of each strip.

6. Right sides facing, sew piping to pillow top.

7. *Pillow back:* Apply fusible interfacing along one 15" edge of each backing piece ¼" from edge; press edge under ¼" and then again 2". Topstitch.

8. Mark positions of three buttonholes along finished edge of orange piece; sew buttonholes. Attach buttons to yellow piece.

9. With pillow back buttoned and right sides facing, sew pillow front to back; turn right side out. Unbutton cover and insert pillow form.

10. Brush chenille with chenille brush, spraying it lightly with water as you brush. Launder to enhance the fluff.

Swirl Pillow

1. From blue fabric cut two 8" squares and one piece 15" x 11";

Mini Geometric Pillow
Enlarge pattern 200% before transferring

cut same pieces from green fabric. Cut two strips 15" x 2" from fusible interfacing.

2. Follow steps 2–10 for daisy pillow, substituting blue and green fabrics, blue piping and blue buttons, and transferring swirl pattern. Apply blueberry chenille to green fabric and limeade chenille to blue fabric.

Mini Geometric Pillow

1. From fabric cut one 10¼" square for front and two 10¼" x 8" pieces for backs. Cut two strips 10¼" x 2" from fusible interfacing.

2. Transfer design to pillow front.

3. Remove tear-away backing from chenille trim; cut into long strips using cutting guide.

4. Sew strips to pillow front, back-tacking at beginning and

end of each strip.

5. Right sides facing, sew piping to pillow top.

6. *Pillow back:* Apply fusible interfacing along one 10¼" edge of each backing piece ¼" from edge; press edge under ¼" and then again 2". Topstitch.

7. Mark positions of three buttonholes along finished edge of one back piece; sew buttonholes. Attach buttons to other back piece.

8. With pillow back buttoned and right sides facing, sew pillow front to back; turn right side out. Unbutton cover and insert pillow form.

9. Brush chenille with chenille brush, spraying it lightly with water as you brush. Launder to enhance the fluff. ✄

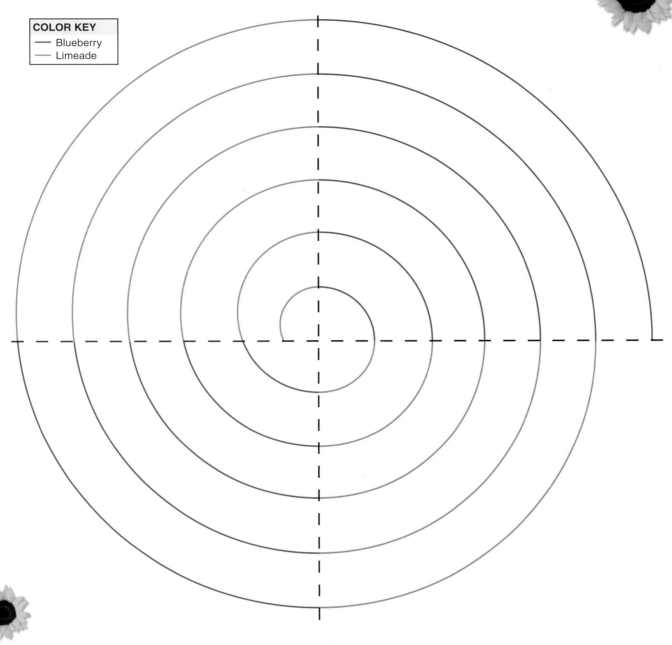

COLOR KEY
— Blueberry
— Limeade

Swirl Pillow
Enlarge pattern 125% before transferring

Summer Potpourri With Panache

Who says potpourri should be made up of only dried flower petals and wood curls? Fill the air with a pleasant scent and use some scraps in a pretty way by creating your own potpourri mix.

Get creative! Add a touch of lace, a button or two, small felt shapes, a snip of metallic thread, miniature wood cutouts, a silk flower or leaf, a bold bead or colorful pompoms. Most of these items act as a fixative, meaning that they can hold scent well.

Just place scraps in a large self-sealing bag and add several drops of essential oil or fragrance oil.

Seal bag and shake, shake, shake!

Give the potpourri a day or two, then place in a bowl. Refresh the mixture by adding drops of scent.

This smells great and adds a touch of merriment to any room. You can even coordinate colors for each season of the year! ✄

Fall Fantasy!

Crafting during autumn can bring satisfaction and make you feel like a professional designer at heart! By using crafting odds and ends along with the motifs found in nature such as autumn leaves and plump pumpkins, you can create one-of-a-kind treasures that will add a cheerful touch to the fall season.

Happy Halloween

Scare up plenty of compliments with this colorful Halloween decoration made from simply painted wood shapes and craft foam remnants.

Design by Lorine Mason

Materials

- Wooden plaques: 3¼" x 5¼" oval, 4" heart
- 6" ¼"-diameter dowel
- Craft foam: purple, yellow, brown, green
- Purple 4¼" x 2" "Happy Halloween" craft foam cutout*
- Wiggly eyes: 2 (7mm), 2 (10mm)
- Green pompoms: 5mm, 10mm
- 24" 24-gauge green plastic-coated craft wire
- Acrylic paints*: lavender, pumpkin
- Satin varnish
- Paintbrush
- Fine- and extra-fine-point permanent black markers
- Tacky craft glue
- Craft drill with ¼" bit

Creative Hands craft foam cutout from Fibre Craft; Americana acrylic paints from DecoArt.

Instructions

1. Drill ⅜"-deep hole in center of oval plaque and in center of heart's curved edge.

2. Paint all surfaces of heart and dowel orange; paint all surfaces of oval lavender; let dry.

3. Using brush handle dipped in orange, add clusters of three dots to lavender plaque; let dry.

4. Apply two coats varnish to all painted pieces; let dry.

5. Referring to patterns, cut one bat from purple craft foam and two leaves from green; cut also a simple 1" stem from brown and two ⅜" x ⅝" ovals from yellow for eyes.

6. Using extra-fine-point marker, draw broken lines down front of heart (pumpkin) to indicate sections; add broken outline around bat and details to wings.

7. Glue small eyes and pompom nose to bat; add smile with extra-fine-point marker. Glue larger eyes to bottoms of yellow foam ovals; glue ovals, larger pompom nose and stem to pumpkin; add smile with fine-point marker.

8. Glue bat to back of pumpkin.

9. Cut 6" piece wire; coil around handle of small paintbrush; bend in half. Punch one end of wire through one leaf; bend to secure. Glue fold in coil at base of pumpkin stem; glue second leaf in place to conceal fold in coil.

10. Glue dowel in holes in plaques for stem. Starting at top, wrap remaining 9" piece of wire around dowel. When you reach bottom, coil remaining wire around paintbrush handle and bend upward. Thread end through foam "Happy Halloween" cutout. ✂

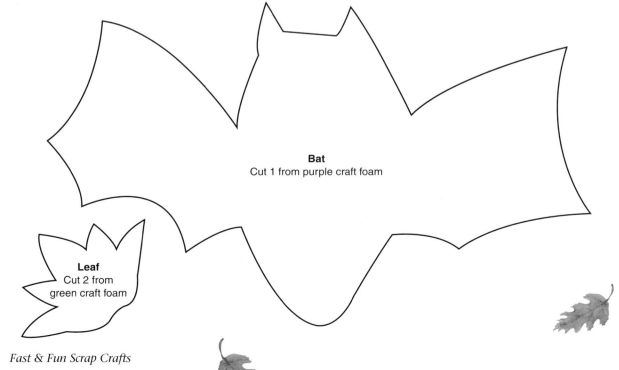

Bat
Cut 1 from purple craft foam

Leaf
Cut 2 from green craft foam

Pumpkin Gift Tote

Even the simplest gifts take on extra panache when presented in homemade carriers like this cheerful tote!

Design by Dorris Sorensen

Materials

- Jewel-tone paints*: citrine yellow, emerald green, golden topaz, onyx, ruby red, smokey brown quartz, white pearl
- Pewter liquid leading*
- White craft glue*
- 5¼" x 8¼" x 4⅝" corrugated paper gift bag with handles
- Brown-paper-bag-colored card stock
- Craft paper: yellow, orange, green
- Decorative paper edgers
- 7" ⅞"-wide black-and-white gingham ribbon
- 1 yard 18-gauge sour apple wire*
- Small paintbrush
- Small piece sponge
- Tracing paper
- Dark graphite paper

**Paint Jewels paints and leading and Sobo glue, all from Delta; Fun Wire from Toner Plastics.*

Instructions

1. Referring to pattern, transfer design to card stock (see "Using Transfer & Graphite Paper" in the General Instructions, page 174).

2. Referring to manufacturer's instructions, apply liquid leading to pattern outlines using gentle, even pressure and keeping lines as even and fine as possible. Let dry completely.

3. Following manufacturer's instructions and applying paints directly from bottles, color in sections: *topaz*—pumpkin; *green*—leaves; *brown*—stem; *yellow*—triangular part of eyes, nose and mouth; *onyx*—right side of eyes; *white*—tooth. Let dry.

4. Add onyx comma strokes over eyes; sponge cheeks with mixture of red and topaz; let dry. Using white, dot highlights on eyes and cheeks. Let dry.

5. Cut out pumpkin, leaving narrow margin around edges of design. Lay shape on yellow paper and trace outline 3⁄16" larger all around; cut out. Lay yellow shape on top of orange and repeat; lay orange sheet on top of green and repeat, cutting green shape with paper edgers. Glue layers together and glue assembled layers to bag.

6. Tie knot in center of ribbon; trim to 4½" long and notch ends; glue to pumpkin shapes.

7. Cut wire in half; wrap one piece around each handle. Run wire ends to outside of bag through holes at base of handles; coil ends around paintbrush handle. ✄

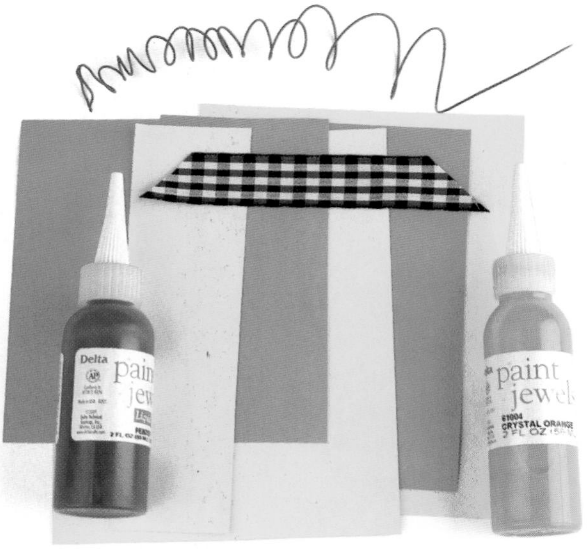

Pumpkin Gift Tote

Jack-o'-Lantern Jar

A used jar takes on new life as a smiling pumpkin to fill with treats!

Design by Betsy H. Edwards

Materials

- Clean, dry 16-ounce glass jar with screw-on lid
- Surface conditioner*
- Paints*: beyond turquoise, apple candy green, cantaloupe, citrus yellow, Mediterranean blue, red iron oxide, royal purple, tangerine, ultra white
- Paintbrushes: #12 flat, #5 round, 10/0 liner
- Natural silk sponge
- White graphite paper

PermEnamel surface conditioner and paints from Delta.

Instructions

1. Referring to manufacturer's instructions, paint jar and lid with surface conditioner.

2. Squeeze silver-dollar-size puddles of cantaloupe and tangerine paint onto palette. Turn jar upside down. Wet sponge; squeeze out excess moisture. Dip sponge into cantaloupe, then tangerine; pounce on paper towel to remove some paint. Pounce sponge all over jar. As needed, redip sponge in paint, always pouncing excess onto paper towel. Continue until jar is completely covered. Let dry, then add a second coat. Let dry.

3. Wash sponge; squeeze out excess moisture. Squeeze quarter-size puddles of turquoise, blue, purple and green onto palette. Using same method as in step 2, pounce colors individually onto lid and rim in that order, rinsing sponge and squeezing out excess moisture between colors.

4. When paint on jar is dry, use pencil to lightly divide jar into four

or six equal sections. Pour quarter-size puddle of red iron oxide onto clean palette. Dip flat brush in water; wipe on edge of water container to remove excess. Put one corner of brush in paint. Stroke brush back and forth on palette so that paint moves across chisel edge of brush—intense color in corner dipped in paint, gradually fading to plain water in opposite corner. With colored corner of brush, paint over vertical lines. Reload brush as needed, blending color back and forth each time. Let dry.

5. Transfer outlines of eyes, nose and mouth (page 105) to jar (see "Using Transfer & Graphite Paper" in the General Instructions, page 174). Paint eyes, nose and mouth yellow using round brush; let dry, then add a second coat. Let dry.

Continued on page 105

Pumpkin Patch Flowerpot

Imagine it dressing up your kitchen windowsill—a small pot of ivy, rosemary, mint or chives tucked in this quick and easy painted planter.

Design by Betsy H. Edwards

Materials

- 3"–3½" terra-cotta flowerpot with saucer
- Satin varnish*
- Acrylic paints*: bittersweet orange, black, jubilee green, opaque yellow, tangerine
- Paintbrushes: 1" sponge brush, 10/0 liner, #4 round, #12 flat shader
- Wooden toothpick (optional)
- Tracing paper
- Gray or white graphite paper

Ceramcoat varnish and paints from Delta.

Instructions

1. Wash flowerpot and saucer; let dry thoroughly. Seal all surfaces with varnish; let dry.

2. Paint exterior of saucer and interior of pot black; let dry. Apply second coat if needed.

3. Paint ½" black stripes on pot rim; using liner, outline stripes with green.

4. Dip handle of liner in tangerine; dot column of four dots in one of the unpainted sections of rim, working from bottom to top. Redip handle and repeat in next unpainted section; repeat around rim. Let dry.

5. Using tip of liner handle or toothpick dipped in bittersweet, apply highlight to each dot.

6. Using liner, paint squiggly black line around pot just below rim.

7. Referring to pattern (page 105), transfer design to side of pot (see "Using Transfer & Graphite Paper" in the General Instructions, page 174).

8. Paint pumpkins bittersweet; paint stems and tendrils green; let dry. Reapply section lines to pumpkins with graphite paper.

9. Wet shader; touch to paper towel until shine is gone from bristles. Dip corner of brush in puddle of tangerine; blend bristles back and forth in same spot on palette. Paint should begin to "walk" across width of bristles, from intense color in one corner to plain water in opposite corner. Place paint end of bristles next to section line on one pumpkin. Using short, choppy strokes, shade to divide pumpkins into sections, rinsing and reloading brush for each section.

Continued on page 105

Stamped "Boo!" Card

Use paper scraps and rubber stamps to create absolutely boo-tiful Halloween greetings!

Design by Vicki Blizzard

Materials

- Card stock: 8½" x 12" sheet each topaz parchment and bright orange, ½ sheet each topaz and ivory
- Deckle paper edgers
- Paper crimper
- Pumpkin stamp set*
- Pigment stamp pads*: alpine, brown, chianti, cocoa, dune, eggplant, evergreen, hunter green, marigold, old rose, orange, ruby, teal, terra cotta, topaz
- Markers*: kiwi, pure orange, pure yellow, rose, spring green, summer sun, wheat
- Pure brown writer*
- ½" and ⅞" white alphabet stickers*
- Glue*
- Paper glaze*
- 26-gauge gold craft wire
- Wire cutters
- Round-nose pliers

Clear Impressions pumpkin stamps #35-9091 from Provo Craft; Color Box Cat's Eye stamp pads from Clearsnap, Inc.; Scroll & Brush markers and writer from EK Success Ltd.; Alphabitties Fat Dot White #42-1513 and #42-1442 Repositionable stickers from Provo Craft; Aleene's 2 in 1 Glue and paper glaze from Duncan.

Project Note

Cut with scissors unless instructed otherwise.

Instructions

1. Cut 10" x 7" topaz parchment; fold in half to make 5" x 7" card, creasing fold.

2. *Card front:* Stamp solid leaf randomly on card front using topaz ink. Randomly stamp card again using leaf overlay stamp and remaining ink colors, stamping over topaz leaves and running designs off edges of card.

3. Using deckle paper edgers, cut orange card stock 1¾" x 8". Run short edge through crimper; glue to card front ¼" from fold.

4. Using brown ink, stamp three frames on topaz card stock; trim just outside edges. Place large B sticker in center of one frame and large O in center of remaining frames. Outline inside and outside of each letter with brown writer. Color leaves on frames using markers in desired fall colors. Glue frames down front of card, left edges aligned with fold.

5. Using brown ink, stamp large pumpkin stack on ivory card stock.

Using markers, color frogs' eyelids and spots kiwi and spring green; color spots, swirls and stars on pumpkins pure orange; color outer stars with summer sun; color leaves in desired fall colors; color centers of outside dots with rose.

6. Cut out stamped pumpkin image slightly beyond edge of stamped design; glue to orange card stock. Using deckle paper edgers, trim orange card stock ¼" from cut edge of stamped image.

7. Cut two 2" pieces wire; wrap one end of each into a spiral using round-nose pliers. Glue straight ends behind ivory layer of stamped image as shown. Glue pumpkin unit to front of card.

8. Apply paper glaze to stars and each leaf on frames and pumpkin; let dry.

9. *Inside:* Using brown ink, stamp pumpkins-in-a-row on ivory card stock; color stems with wheat marker and dots with pure orange.

Color leaves in desired colors.

10. Using deckle edgers, cut 3¾" x 3¼" orange card stock. Glue stamped pumpkins-in-a-row to card stock ½" from bottom.

11. Using smaller alphabet stickers, spell "Happy Haunting!" above pumpkins on orange card stock. Glue inside card. ✄

Jack-o'-Lantern Jar

Jack-o'-Lantern Jar

Continued from page 102

6. Using liner and purple, outline eyes, nose and mouth with short, wiggly lines; paint wiggly broken line around rim of lid.

7. Dry-brush red iron oxide onto eyes, nose and mouth where indicated by short lines on pattern: Dip round brush in paint, then remove

most of paint by brushing back and forth on paper towel. Gently stroke almost-dry brush onto jar.

8. Using liner, add white highlights where indicated by dots and comma strokes.

9. Using same method as in step 7, dry-brush yellow down center of each section of pumpkin.

10. Let jar cure for 10 days before washing. ✄

Pumpkin Patch Flowerpot

Continued from page 103

10. Turn saucer upside down so black surface faces you. Using liner throughout, paint squiggly tangerine circle near center of top.

11. Just below top, paint thin, horizontal, bittersweet line; cross with ⅜"-long perpendicular tangerine lines every ⅛".

12. Paint green checkerboard pattern on rim; paint green squiggly circles along top and bottom of tangerine lines painted in step 11.

13. Using tip of toothpick or liner brush handle dipped in tangerine, apply dot in every other square on rim; dot bittersweet in remaining squares. Let all paints dry.

14. Apply two coats varnish to all surfaces, letting varnish dry between coats. ✄

Pumpkin Patch Flowerpot

"Boo!" Jacket

Use fabric paints and stencils to create a lightweight jacket perfect for those unpredictable fall afternoons.

Design by Phyllis Sandford

Materials

- Black cotton long-sleeved shirt
- Orange cotton embroidery floss
- #18 tapestry needle
- Stencils*: Halloween spider, Halloween night, 2" dot alphabet, trick-or-treat
- Aerosol stencil adhesive*
- Stencil buddy*
- Orange fabric dye*
- Shimmering fabric colors*: egg yolk, leaf green, white
- Small pieces of stencil sponge
- Palette paper
- Shirt-painting board

Spooky Stencils Halloween Spider #88-136-0310 and Halloween Night #88-132-0310, Stencil Magic 2" Whimsical Dot Alphabet #95-623-0018, Cherished Memories Trick or Treat stencil #60-228-0911, stencil adhesive, Stencil Buddy, Starlite Shimmering Fabric Colors and Fabric Dye all from Delta.

Instructions

1. Wash and dry shirt without using fabric softener. Cut shirt up center front; place on shirt-painting board.

2. Using 6 strands floss, blanket-stitch around neck and down front edges, turning cut edges under ¼"–½".

3. Peel backing from spider stencil. Place pumpkin kitty-corner on right side of jacket front near top. Using stencil buddy and sponge, stencil pumpkin with orange dye, pouncing excess color onto palette paper before stenciling shirt. Using a clean piece of sponge for each color, use same method to stencil leaves with green and face with egg yolk paints.

4. Place pumpkin from Halloween night stencil under the first at an angle. Stencil pumpkin, leaves and face as in step 3.

5. Add a third pumpkin below second as in step 3.

6. Using Halloween night stencil and egg yolk paint, stencil stars randomly on front of shirt.

7. Spray back of alphabet stencil with adhesive. Place the letters "BOO" just above hemline in middle of side; stencil with white.

8. Repeat steps 3–7 on left side of shirt.

9. Spray back of trick-or-treat stencil with adhesive; center pumpkin over "BOO" on left side only. Stencil pumpkin with orange, leaves with green and ghost with white.

10. Let paint dry per manufacturer's instructions before wearing or laundering. ✄

Yo-Yo Yeah!

As a kid you might have played with a yo-yo made of wood or plastic. But the yo-yos I'm talking about are circles of fabric that are gathered firmly along the edges to form circles of fabric.

These yo-yos are used to make beautiful quilts, dolls and Christmas ornaments, and to embellish just about everything from blankets to wreaths. Yo-yos are fun because you can use scraps of fabric to create a project immediately, or store the yo-yos for future projects. Yo-yos are also fun to embellish with buttons, charms, yarn or ribbon bows and other trims.

Simply make a circle template from cardboard or other heavyweight paper or lightweight plastic. (I recommend making templates ranging in size from 1½"–4" in diameter for variety.) Use any type of thread. Sew on embellishments or attach them with glue.

Framed Leaf Print

Dress up a cast-off frame with sponge-painted colors and beads.

Design by June Fiechter

Materials

- Recycled 8" x 10" frame
- Drill and ⅛" bit
- Orange plastic-coated wire*
- Vellum die-cut leaf*
- 4mm beads: red clay, moss*
- White scrapbook paper
- Sponge brush
- Black transfer paper
- Acrylic paints*: camel, coffee bean, lime light, olive green dark
- Soft cloth
- Varnish*
- Tacky craft glue*

Toner Plastics wire, Paper Reflections leaf from DMD Industries, beads from The Beadery, FolkArt paints and varnish from Plaid, Crafter's Pick Ultimate Tacky Glue from API.

Instructions

1. In middle of top of frame, drill a row of three holes, 1" apart. About ¼" above this row, drill two holes 1" apart, staggering their positions relative to the first row of holes. Repeat in center bottom of frame, drilling row of three holes above row of two holes.

2. Down center of each side of frame, drill a row of five holes each 1" apart. About ¼" outside each row, drill a row of four holes 1" apart, again staggering their positions relative to the first row.

3. *Paint frame:* Blot on camel paint with sponge, then lime, then olive. Let dry, then rub on small amount of coffee paint with soft cloth. Let dry.

4. Coat frame with varnish, keeping holes open.

5. Run wire zigzag fashion from hole to hole, threading on three beads—red clay, moss, red clay—between each pair of holes and twisting wire ends on back. Add a drop of glue.

6. Cut paper to fit in frame; glue leaf to center of paper and mount in frame. ✂

Autumn Oven Mitt

What a clever way to dress up your kitchen or breakfast nook for the fall season! It's great for using worn or too-thin mitts, too; just turn the spot or burn mark to the back!

Design by Florence Bolen Tebbets

Materials

- Oven mitt
- Lightweight cardboard cut from cereal box
- Polyester fiberfill
- Coordinating chenille stem
- Serrated knife
- 4" block floral foam
- Silk fall leaves
- Silk mini sunflowers
- 6–8 fall picks including pumpkins, gourds, nuts, pods, berries, etc.
- Red enamel apple
- Mini bunch grapes
- Novelty wooden birdhouse pick
- 2 small mushroom birds
- Novelty shovel and pitchfork
- Low-temperature glue gun
- Wire cutters

Instructions

1. Trace around mitt onto cardboard, omitting thumb. Cut out; trim to fit inside mitt.

2. In front of cardboard, lightly stuff mitt with fiberfill, stopping 3" from top. Stuff just enough to give front of mitt nicely rounded appearance.

3. *Hanger:* Bend chenille stem into loop; twist ends together. Glue ends of loop between back of mitt and cardboard.

4. Use serrated knife to cut foam to fit in top of mitt; glue to cardboard.

5. Apply glue to stems of picks, flowers and leaves before inserting them in foam. Insert leaves for background, then sunflowers, then pumpkin and berry picks, allowing some of the berries to "spill" down mitt. Glue apple at center front; add grapes.

6. Glue birdhouse at center back, extending above leaves. Glue one bird to birdhouse and one to sunflowers; glue pitchfork and shovel between leaves and vegetables. ✄

Mosaic Leaf Stones

Here's a unique way to showcase special beads, buttons and other odds and ends!
The resulting leaves make lovely paperweights or garden stones!

Designs by Sarah Donnelly

Materials

Oak Leaf

- 8 (¾") copper-color glass "nuggets"
- 4" 10-gauge copper wire or ⅛" tubing
- Metal 4½" x 2½" oak leaf cookie cutter with rounded corners

Maple Leaf

- Assorted glass (not plastic) beads
- Metal 6" x 5" maple leaf cookie cutter

Each Leaf

- Stone mix* or premixed concrete without gravel
- Paper
- Pencil with eraser
- Duct tape
- Dishwashing liquid
- Small paintbrush
- Tin snips
- Waxed paper
- Rigid cookie sheet or board
- Dust mask
- Rubber gloves
- Disposable plastic containers (cottage cheese cartons, etc.)
- 1 tablespoon measuring spoon
- Craft stick
- Bucket of water
- Spray bottle of water
- Small, old screwdriver
- Toothbrush
- Scouring pad
- Paper clip
- Sponge
- Sanding block
- Small cork or felt pads

StoneCraft Mix from Milestones Products.

Constructing Mosaics

1. Trace cookie cutter on paper. Lay out design on paper pattern:

Oak leaf: Form S-curve in wire; lay in center. Arrange nuggets, leaving ⅛"–¼" between nuggets and pattern edge.

Maple leaf: Arrange beads; for "veins," place beads of same color close together. Leave ⅛"–¼" between beads and pattern edge.

2. Open cookie cutter at stem with tin snips. Tape seam together on outside; use paintbrush to lightly coat inside of cookie cutter with dishwashing liquid.

3. Lay cutter on waxed paper on cookie sheet, making sure cutter sits flat.

4. Put on dust mask and gloves. Gently empty dry mix—¼ cup for oak leaf, ¾ cup for maple leaf—into disposable mixing bowl. Using craft stick, stir in water—1 tablespoon for oak leaf, 2 tablespoons for maple leaf—and blend thoroughly. Blend to consistency of thick, sticky cookie batter, adding water a few drops at a time as needed and blending very thoroughly after each addition. (Runny, soupy mixtures will not harden.)

5. Fill cookie cutter with even, ¾"-thick layer of mixture. You now have about 50 minutes to complete your mosaic. Remove mask; use craft stick or gloved finger to compress and spread out mix, gently jiggling cookie sheet to smooth surface.

6. Take the time *now* to rinse tools in bucket of water. Set bucket aside to settle overnight. ***Note:*** *Do not rinse or pour mix down drains, as it may clog pipes.*

7. Transfer mosaic design, laying wire and glass nuggets—or beads—on top of wet surface; maintain ⅛"–¼" margin around edge.

8. Push all pieces straight down with eraser end of pencil until they are embedded more than halfway. Go over entire design several times, evening out surface. (Small amounts of wet stone on the mosaic will clean up easily later, but the neater you work now, the less cleanup you will need to do.) Clean up any mix that seeps out under cookie cutter.

9. Set piece aside for 24 hours; spray surface with water in spray bottle and set aside for another 24 hours.

10. After a day or two, dispose of water and concrete in bucket (step 6) by pouring clear water into yard and disposing of concrete sludge in garbage.

Finishing

1. *Clean surface:* Put on gloves and safety glasses. Work carefully, as hardened stone can still crumble. Clean beads by dipping toothbrush or scouring pad in water and gently scrubbing entire surface until excess concrete lifts off. Use as much water as needed and remove excess with sponge. If needed, gently scrape concrete from nuggets/beads and nugget/bead edges with sharp tip of opened paper clip to reveal more and give crisper outline.

2. *Unmold leaf:* Lift cookie cutter; remove waxed paper. Set down and carefully loosen cutter, opening and bending as little as possible. If stuck, use paper clip to carefully scrape top and bottom edges where stone comes in contact with cutter. Remove cutter, lifting it up or opening it all the way.

3. Use shaft of screwdriver to scrape and smooth crusty edges. Rinse leaf in water; leave to cure for a few more days.

4. Smooth edges with sanding block as needed. Glue cork or felt pads to bottom. ✂

Calorie-Free Candy Jar

Enjoy all the appeal of an old-fashioned candy jar filled with treats—without the dieter's guilt!

Design by Kay Davis

Materials

- Glass candy jar with lid
- Assorted colors of yarn
- Cellophane*
- Pencil
- Vise
- Hot-glue gun
- Thread (optional)

Look for cellophane in your craft store's cake decorating department.

Round Candies

1. Wrap a ball of yarn to measure ¾"; glue yarn end.

2. Repeat to make candies in quantity and colors desired.

Pinwheel Candies

1. Secure pencil upright in vise.

2. Cut 36" each of red and white yarn (or any two colors); fold each in half.

3. Slip loops over pencil; hold white off to right and red off to left. Twist white yarn to the right several times; cross over red yarn. Twist red yarn several times; pass back over white. Repeat until you reach ends of yarn; glue to hold.

4. Wind yarn in pinwheel to measure 1" (double layer of yarn may be necessary for thickness). Glue.

5. Repeat to make candies in quantity and colors desired.

Finishing

1. Wrap each candy in 3½" square of cellophane, twisting ends in opposite directions. Secure knots with thread if cellophane twists will not stay closed.

2. Fill jar with candies. ✂

Stacked Decoupage Boxes

Distinctive crackle-finish lids and touches of gold make this a most appealing accent piece!

Design by Dorothy Egan

Materials

- Round papier-mâché boxes*: 3½", 3¾" and 4¼" diameter
- Printed paper napkins
- 4 (¾") wooden candle cups
- Acrylic craft paints* in 3 or 4 colors to complement napkin prints (see Project Notes)
- Paintbrushes: ½", 1" wash, #6 blender
- Matte decoupage coating*
- Crackle medium*
- Antiquing glaze (optional)
- Soft cloth (optional)
- Botanicals: small nest, gold eggs or pods, dried flowers or grasses
- 1 yard wired ribbon
- Craft glue
- Hot-glue gun

Boxes from D&CC; Americana paints from DecoArt; Mod Podge decoupage coating and crackle medium from Plaid.

Project Note

Lilac, deep burgundy, sand and midnite blue paints were used on sample.

Lids

1. Paint box lids burgundy or desired dark color. When dry, apply crackle medium, following manufacturer's instructions. Let dry.

2. When crackle medium is dry enough, paint lids sand. Let dry and crackle. If darker color is desired, apply antiquing glaze, wiping off excess with soft cloth. Let dry completely.

Boxes

1. Separate napkins; discard bottom unprinted layer. Tear motifs from printed layer, tearing one piece ½" larger all around than box bottom and strips wide enough to cover box sides.

2. Paint box bottom and ½" up sides with heavy, even coat of decoupage coating. Apply tissue to wet surface, smoothing wrinkles with soft brush. Paint box sides with decoupage coating; apply more tissue, piecing together smaller pieces as needed to cover box completely. Set aside to dry; cover remaining boxes in same manner.

Assembly

1. *Feet:* Paint candle cups in a splotchy fashion with complementary colors (sample used burgundy, lilac and blue). Let dry. Glue open ends to bottom of largest box.

2. Apply a final coat of decoupage coating to boxes and feet; let dry.

3. Place lids on boxes. Tie bow in center of ribbon. Stack boxes; place bow on top and tie ribbon ends under bottom box, securing with glue.

4. Glue gold eggs in nest; glue nest and dried flowers over bow. ✄

Decoupaged Suitcase

Vintage suitcases are everywhere these days! Our delightful version not only can stand on its own good looks, but also offers handy storage space for linens, towels or out-of-season clothes.

Design by Dorothy Egan

Materials

- Old suitcase
- Wrapping paper, decoupage papers, sheet music, postcards, photos
- Lace, buttons, charms
- Acrylic paints* to match/coordinate with suitcase: antique gold metallic, celery green, lamp black
- 4 paper clock faces*
- Paints*: earth brown, golden halo, shadow tan
- Matte decoupage coating*
- Thick white glue*
- Paintbrushes: 1" flat or foam, #1 script, #2 flat
- Matte finish*
- Sea sponge
- Stylus
- Matches
- Masking tape
- Hot-glue gun

Clock faces from Walnut Hollow; Americana acrylic paints and Heavenly Hues paints from DecoArt; Mod Podge decoupage coating from Plaid; Crafter's Pick The Ultimate! Glue from API; Krylon matte finish.

Project Notes

Vintage photos, sheet music, post-cards and other paper memorabilia can be photocopied in color, and the copies applied to the suitcase.

For an aged look, wipe a sponge containing very little gold or tan paint across papers or lace; paper edges can also be singed with a match.

Consider how you will display the suitcase; apply lettering so it will read right side up.

Painting

1. Wash luggage well with water and mild detergent; let dry. Spray areas to be painted with matte finish; let dry.

2. Paint suitcase *except* binding and hardware celery green; let dry.

3. Wet sponge; squeeze dry, and lightly sponge painted areas with brown.

Decorations

1. Using script brush and lamp black paint thinned with a little water, write lettering on suitcase as desired; sample has "Take Time for the Memories" on one side. Let dry, then repeat with gold paint.

2. Position two clock faces close to lettering; arrange other design elements on suitcase.

3. Attach design elements by applying decoupage coating to back of each piece and pressing firmly in place, working out any bubbles.

4. Paint hands on clock faces with liner and black paint; let dry.

5. Apply thin layer of decoupage coating over surface.

6. Repeat on bottom and remaining sides of suitcase, adding lace, buttons, charms, etc.

7. Apply several more coats decoupage coating, painting around charms and buttons and letting it dry between coats.

8. *Optional interior decoration:* Hot-glue flowers, lace and ribbon inside suitcase as desired. ✂

Fun & Fancy Napkin Rings

The simplest napkins become table fashion statements when they're embraced by rings like these, fashioned from your crafting leftovers!

Designs by Paula Bales

Materials

Each Beaded Ring

- 1" ring cut from cardboard tube from bathroom tissue or paper towels
- Silver 26-gauge paddle wire*
- Wire cutters
- Needle-nose pliers
- About 200 large, multicolored rocaille beads*

Each Button Ring

- 12" 18-gauge silver armature wire*
- Wire cutters
- Needle-nose pliers
- 55 assorted ³⁄₁₆"–½" flat buttons

Fibre Craft Bright paddle wire; beads from Create A Craft; Craft Armature Wire from Plaid.

Beaded Ring

1. Cut cardboard ring open; wrap cardboard strip closely with wire down its entire length. Cut and secure wire end.

2. Secure one end of another 3-yard piece of wire to one end of cardboard; string about 200 beads on wire.

3. Wrap beaded wire around wire-covered cardboard, positioning beads randomly on outside of cardboard.

4. Bend wired, beaded cardboard into ring, overlapping ends; wrap end of beaded wire around overlap to secure.

Button Ring

1. Thread buttons onto wire.

2. Curl each end of wire into a flat coil using needle-nose pliers.

3. Form ring by twisting wire ends together so that coils lie flat across top. ✂

Acorn Purse

Embossed felt adds a touch of realistic texture to this clever fashion accessory!

Design by June Fiechter

Materials

- Embossed felt*: butterscotch, walnut
- Coordinating fabric scraps, including remnant for lining
- Hook-and-loop fastener
- 36" coordinating twisted cording
- Natural raffia
- 2 flat wooden buttons
- Textile adhesive*
- Pinking shears
- Brown sewing thread
- Needle or sewing machine
- Iron

Kunin embossed felt; Aleene's Platinum Bond Super Fabric textile adhesive from Duncan.

Project Notes

Use ⅛"–3⁄16" seam allowance throughout. Use photocopier to enlarge patterns 133 percent before cutting.

Instructions

1. Using scissors, cut two acorn caps from butterscotch felt, two acorns from walnut and two lining pieces from lining fabric.

2. Using pinking shears, cut fabric patches; arrange and sew to front of acorn and cap. Sew acorns together down sides, wrong sides facing, leaving top open.

3. Sew lining pieces together right sides facing, leaving top open. Do not turn right side out, but fold down ½" cuff; press. Slide lining pocket inside acorn and slipstitch fold of lining just below top of acorn.

4. Glue ends of cord inside top corners of acorn.

5. Pin caps in place, overlapping acorns. Sew caps to acorns; sew

caps to each other along sides up to points indicated by dots on pattern. Continue stitching around top of each cap, leaving top of purse open.

6. Glue or stitch fastener pieces inside stems.

7. Glue small raffia bow and one button to patches on acorn; glue button to patches on cap. ✄

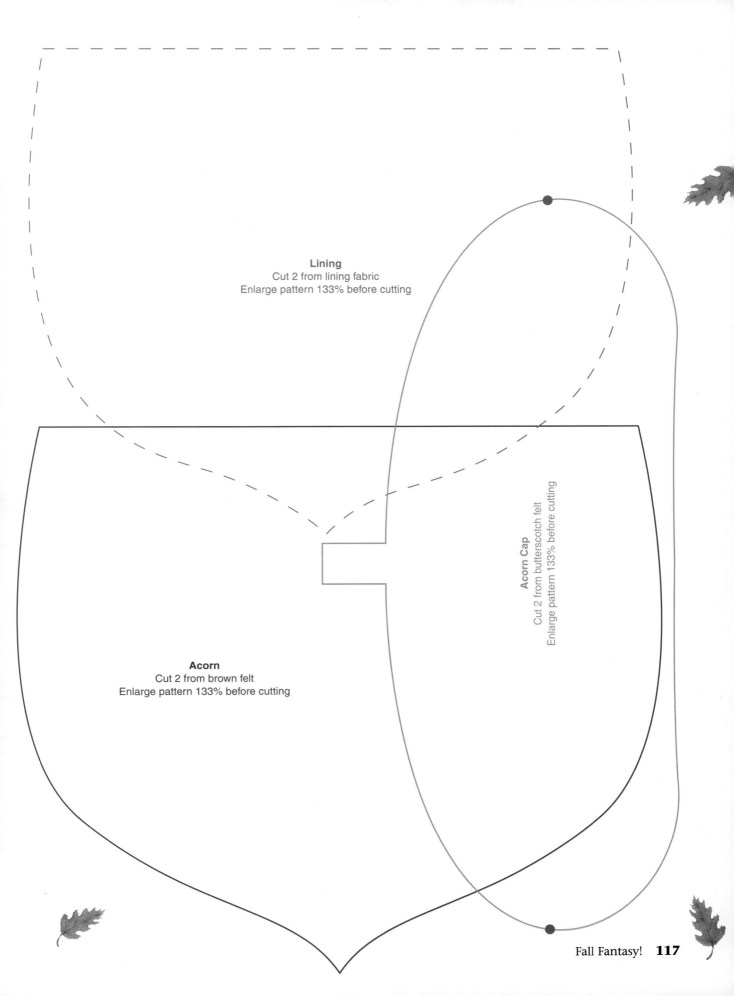

Lining
Cut 2 from lining fabric
Enlarge pattern 133% before cutting

Acorn Cap
Cut 2 from butterscotch felt
Enlarge pattern 133% before cutting

Acorn
Cut 2 from brown felt
Enlarge pattern 133% before cutting

Free-Form Wire Frame

Beads and charms dangle delightfully from a fun frame decorated with wire coils and glass nuggets.

Design by Katie Hacker

Materials

- Unfinished 8" x 10" wooden frame with 3"-wide sides*
- Silver wire*: 2½ yards 16-gauge, 18" 20-gauge
- 1" foam paintbrush
- Wedgwood green acrylic paint*
- Acrylic matte varnish*
- Sawtooth picture hanger
- Assorted glass, gemstone and silver 4mm–10mm beads*
- 1" silver frame charm*
- Silver jewelry findings*: jump rings, head pins
- 4 (16-gauge) silver eye screws
- 7 (16-gauge) silver staples
- 8 iridescent clear glass flat marbles
- Wire cutters
- Round-nose and flat-nose pliers
- Sandpaper
- Hammer
- Super glue
- Craft drill with ⅟₁₆" bit

Timeless Frames unfinished craft frame; Beadalon Colourcraft wire and findings; Ceramcoat paint and varnish from Delta; glass beads from Hands of the Hills and Hirschberg Schutz & Co.; Halcraft USA gemstone beads; frame charm from Creative Beginnings.

Instructions

1. Attach sawtooth hanger to back of frame. Sand frame; wipe off dust and seal with one coat varnish; let dry.

2. Paint frame with a wash of one part paint and two parts water. Let dry, then seal with a second coat of varnish; let dry.

3. Cut 16-gauge wire into 16", 32" and 42" pieces.

4. Form loop at one end of each piece with round-nose pliers, then shape as shown. For coils, use fingers to turn end loop and form coil.

5. Arrange wire pieces on front of frame. Drill pilot holes for staples, then place staples in holes over wire and hammer in place.

6. Drill pilot hole for one screw in left side of frame 4" from top and 1½" in from outside. Drill three more holes in bottom edge 4½" in from right edge and 1½" apart. Screw screws into holes.

7. Make four dangling charms, threading on beads as desired, and attaching a jump ring at top of each. Suspend frame charm from bottom of one charm; hang from eye screw on left side. Suspend remaining charms from eye screws in bottom of frame.

8. Glue marbles to frame. ✁

Wire Coil Clock

Odds and ends of craft wire are coiled into curlicues to dress up this stylish, versatile timepiece.

Design by Katie Hacker

Materials

- 6½" x 8½" oval wooden clock*
- 2½" x 3½" gold clock face/movement*
- 1½ yards 20-gauge gold wire*
- 1" foam paintbrush
- 16" 16-gauge copper wire*
- #10 flat paintbrush
- Acrylic paints*: metallic gold, black
- Acrylic matte varnish*
- Sawtooth picture hanger
- Wire cutters
- Round-nose and flat-nose pliers
- Sandpaper
- Hammer
- Super glue

Clock and face/movement from Walnut Hollow; Beadalon Colourcraft wire; Ceramcoat paints and varnish from Delta.

Instructions

1. Attach sawtooth hanger to back of clock. Sand clock; wipe off dust and seal with one coat varnish; let dry.

2. Using foam brush, paint clock front black; using flat brush, paint edge gold. Let dry, then seal with varnish; let dry.

3. Cut gold wire into five 9" pieces and eight 6" pieces.

4. *Bend each 9" piece into a 2¼"–2⅜" S-curve:* Form loop at one end with round-nose pliers. Turn loop with fingers, forming loose coil. For other end of S, bend coil in opposite direction. Flatten each end with hammer. Glue S-curves to clock.

5. *Bend each 6" piece into tight coil:* Form loop at one end with round-nose pliers. Grasp loop with flat-nose pliers and turn to form coil. Hammer each coil flat and glue to clock.

6. Cut copper wire into four 4" pieces. Shape each into a loose coil; glue to clock.

7. Mount clock face and movement in clock. ✀

"Stained-Glass" Note Cards

Color vellum in bright designs to create this pair of dazzling cards.

Designs by Bev George

Materials
Each Card
- Blank card with matching envelope
- ½ sheet dotted vellum*
- Permanent markers*
- Gold or silver metallic paper or card stock (optional)
- Craft knife
- Paper edgers (optional)

White dot Parchlucent vellum by Paper Adventures; Blank Expressions markers from Highsmith.

Coloring

1. Trace desired pattern on vellum with black marker (or, copy pattern by running vellum through dry toner photocopying machine).

2. Color design as desired on back of vellum; let dry.

3. Turn over and color desired areas on front of card. Coloring both sides intensifies areas and vellum becomes transparent. Coloring the back only leaves a "frosted" appearance, and white dots remain very apparent.

Assembly

Option A—Pumpkin Harvest: Fold card in half; cut 4" x 2½" opening in front. Cut out colored vellum

Pumpkin Harvest

Buttoned-Up Frame

This clever frame is constructed using a recycled CD box!

Design by Paula Bales

Materials

- Recycled clear CD box, with spindle insert removed
- All-purpose joint compound
- Small putty knife
- Assorted ¼"–1" buttons

Instructions

1. Measure a 1¼" border around outside on front of CD box. Using putty knife, smooth joint compound onto border area.

2. Push buttons into compound; let dry completely.

3. Tape photo inside CD box.

4. Open frame to stand easel-fashion on table. Or, close frame to hang from wall. ✂

"Stained-Glass" Note Cards

design and glue behind opening.

Option B—Patriotic Thanks: Fold card in half; trim ⁵⁄₁₆" from long edge of front only using scissors or paper edgers. Cut 3½" x 4½" metallic paper for liner. Glue colored vellum design in center of liner; glue to front of card. Glue 1"-wide strip metallic paper along exposed inner edge. ✂

Patriotic Thanks

Tin Pumpkin Accent

*Perched on a giant "spring," this perky pumpkin adds
a bright splash of fall color to a mantel, bookcase or countertop.*

Design by June Fiechter

Materials

- Large empty tin juice can
- Utility cutter* or tin snips
- Soft aluminum modeling wire*
- White polymer clay*
- Craft glue*
- Metal paints*: bright gold, bright yellow, espresso bean, real red, true green
- 11 fall berries on stems
- 3 silk leaves
- 2 (6") pieces copper wire*
- Natural raffia
- Paper
- Baking sheet
- Oven

Utility cutter from Fiskars; WireForm Armature Modeling Wire #50070W and Fimo Soft Polymer Clay from Amaco; Crafter's Pick Ultimate Tacky Glue from API; No-Prep Metal Paints Holiday Accents pack from DecoArt; wire from Artistic Wire.

Instructions

1. Cut coil of aluminum wire in half; reserve one piece for another use. Stretch remaining coil, widening base and narrowing top.

2. Roll quarter-block of clay into a long snake; wind around top of coil.

3. Cut can open and flatten it. Referring to pattern, cut pumpkin so stripes run vertically.

4. Press base of pumpkin into clay coil to make groove; remove. Pry groove open about ¼". Set wire with clay on paper on baking sheet; bake according to manufacturer's instructions; let cool.

5. Partially blend yellow and red paints to make orange; paint both sides of pumpkin. Paint stem espresso. Paint wire coil and clay with alternating strokes of green and gold. Let dry.

6. Glue pumpkin in groove; let dry.

7. Tie a strand or two of raffia around stem(s) of nine berries; glue leaf and berries in groove in front of pumpkin. Glue another leaf in groove behind pumpkin.

8. Tie raffia in bow around stem. Coil copper wire around paintbrush; tuck into bow at stem, securing with glue. Glue remaining leaf and berries at stem. ✄

Tin Pumpkin Accent

Fall Frame to Fall in Love With

Any frame will work for this quick craft, but do use a glue designed for the frame material. Jewelry glue is usually a good choice.

By Maria Nerius

Choose a *picture frame* and appropriate *glue.* Collect all your *crafting scraps in fall colors*— browns, oranges, yellows, golds and reds. *Felts, fabrics, craft foam*— nearly anything is a possibility.

Now, start gluing items randomly to the frame, attaching smooth scraps first, then dimensional scraps. You can cut leaf shapes from fabric, felt or craft foam. Wrap the frame with *threads* here and there; add a pretty *button* or *charm.*

Let frame dry, then slide your favorite photo into the frame. ✄

Happy Harvest Turkey

Nothing complicated here. But the results are delightful: a holiday gobbler who is happy to preside over your "Turkey Day" festivities!

Design by Lorine Mason

Materials

- Wooden plaques: 3¼" x 5¼" rectangle, 4" heart
- 2 (4") ¼"-diameter dowels
- 7 wooden craft spoons
- Craft foam: beige, black, red, orange, yellow
- 2 (7mm) wiggly eyes
- 2 (9") pieces 24-gauge green plastic-coated craft wire
- Acrylic paints*: cadmium yellow, country red, pumpkin, sable brown
- Satin varnish
- Paintbrush
- Natural raffia
- 3 (1¼") pumpkins
- Extra-fine-point permanent black marker
- Tacky craft glue
- Craft drill with ¼" bit

Americana acrylic paints from DecoArt.

Instructions

1. Find and mark center in surface of rectangular plaque and top edge of heart plaque. Mark two other positions on each piece, ½" out from center point on each side. Drill ⅜"-deep hole at each of these four side positions.

2. Paint beveled edge of rectangle pumpkin; paint all other surfaces on both plaques brown; let dry.

3. Paint dowels and three spoons yellow; paint two spoons red and two spoons pumpkin; let dry.

4. Apply two coats varnish to all painted pieces; let dry.

5. Referring to patterns, cut two wings, reversing one, from beige craft foam, wattle from red, hat and boots from black, and hatband from yellow; cut also two ¼" squares from yellow for shoe buckles, and ³⁄₁₆" triangle from orange for beak.

6. Using marker, draw "stitching lines" around spoons, wings,

beak, wattle and heart plaque; draw buckle in center of hatband.

7. Glue hat, hatband, wings, beak, wattle and eyes to front of plaque; glue spoons to back for feathers, alternating colors; glue buckles to boots.

8. Glue dowels in holes in plaques for legs. Starting at tops, wrap a 9" piece of wire around each leg. When you reach bottom of leg, coil remaining wire around paintbrush handle and bend upward. Glue boots to fronts of legs.

9. Cut raffia in pieces to resemble straw; glue to base behind turkey. Glue pumpkins on top of straw. ✄

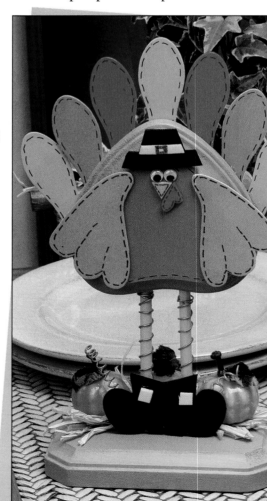

Hat
Cut 1 from
black craft foam

Wing
Cut 2, reversing 1,
from beige craft foam

Boots
Cut 1 from black craft foam

Hatband
Cut 1 from yellow craft foam

Wattle
Cut 1 from red craft foam

"Give Thanks" Turkey

Here's a fine project for practicing your sculpting skills. His "feathers" are silk fall leaves!

Design by Ginny Baker

Materials

- Polymer clay*: black, caramel, Indian red, sunflower yellow, tropical green
- Silk fall leaves: 2 (3"), 2 (2"), 3 (1")
- Cookie cutters: 1" heart, 1" star
- 2 black 1⁄16" ball-head pins
- White tacky glue
- White gel pen
- Needle tool
- 2 toothpicks
- Wire cutters
- Rolling pin or acrylic brayer
- Baking sheet
- Plain white paper
- Ruler or circle template
- Oven

Fimo Soft polymer clay from Amaco.

Project Notes

Clean hands well when changing colors of clay; baby wipes work well. Do not use a rolling pin that has been used with polymer clay for food preparation.

Instructions

1. *Body:* Roll 1¼" ball caramel clay into rounded cone. Use needle tool to impress lines as shown.

2. *Legs:* Break one toothpick in half; stick one half in each side at lower end of body. From yellow clay roll two ⅜" balls, two ½" balls and two ¼" balls; flatten each slightly. Press ⅜" ball onto toothpick on each side of body; press ½" ball onto each ⅜" ball, and ¼" ball onto each ½" ball.

3. *Feet:* Roll yellow clay ⅛" thick; cut two 1" stars. Press two lower points together on each and round off bottoms; round off remaining points

and press onto ends of legs. Use needle tool to add details as shown.

4. *Wings:* Roll two 1" balls caramel into tapered logs; flatten to form wings. Use needle tool to make lines and creases in center of each as shown. Attach wider ends to body.

5. *Head:* Break remaining toothpick in half; insert one half point up into top of body. Roll 1" ball caramel clay into rounded cone; press onto end of toothpick. For beak, form ⅝6" ball yellow into rounded diamond; use head of pin to indent as shown. Press lower half onto face; fold top over slightly. Cut heads from pins; press into face for eyes. Roll ¼" ball red into teardrop for wattle; attach across top of beak. Use needle tool to indent detail lines.

6. *Hat:* Flatten ¾" ball black; press onto head for brim. Form ¾" ball black into rectangle for crown; press onto brim. Roll ⅜" ball green into rope; flatten to ¼" wide and wrap around hat crown. Roll ¼" ball

yellow into rope; shape in square for buckle and press into place.

7. *Bow tie:* Flatten green clay to 1⁄16" thick; cut two ½" rectangles. Pinch ends together; press onto neck with needle tool for bow-tie halves. Roll small ball of green and press to center of tie for knot; indent with needle tool.

8. *Heart:* Flatten red clay to ⅛" thick; cut 1" heart. Attach between wing tips.

9. Line baking sheet with white paper. Place turkey on paper and bake in preheated 265-degree oven for 45 minutes; let cool completely.

10. *Tail:* Glue 2" leaf in center of 3" leaf and 1" leaf in center of 2" leaf; repeat. Glue one section to back of body on each side. Glue remaining 1" leaf to top center of tail between sections.

11. Using gel pen, write "Give Thanks" on heart and add *tiny* highlight to each eye. ✄

Thanksgiving Table Trimmers

Autumn's warm colors dress up any table with a collection of accents featuring seasonal fabrics and motifs cut from paper napkins.

Designs by Bev George

Materials

- Paper napkins with Thanksgiving and fall designs
- Glossy decoupage medium*
- 1 yard autumn-print fabric
- 1" soft paintbrush

Candles

- Pillar candles: 4" x 6", 3" x 3"
- Glitter: "diamond dust" and fine, clear, polyester fabric glitter

Candle Holders

- Terra-cotta flowerpots with saucers: 2 (3") pots *plus* one 3" saucer for 3" holder; 6" and 4" pots with saucers for larger holders
- Chenille stems
- 1" buttons

Floral Centerpiece

- 4" or 6" terra-cotta flowerpot
- Fall florals and berries
- Green floral foam

Place Markers

- 2" terra-cotta flowerpots
- Oven-shrink plastic sheet
- Gold glitter dimensional fabric paint
- 1" buttons

Napkin Rings

- Yellow craft foam
- Natural raffia

Mod Podge from Plaid.

Napkin Technique

1. Separate layers of napkins; use only top printed layer. Carefully cut out motif.

2. Apply thin layer of decoupage medium to surface to which napkin motif will be applied. While medium is still wet, carefully position paper motif on top.

3. Carefully coat paper motif with another layer of decoupage medium.

Candles

1. Referring to Napkin Technique, apply motif(s) to pillar candles as desired.

2. While still wet, sprinkle candle with diamond dust; let dry.

3. Brush off excess diamond dust.

3" Candle Holders

1. Connect two 3" pots by setting them end on end, threading a chenille stem through the holes, and wrapping each end around/through a button in each pot to hold pots together snugly.

2. Top with 3" saucer turned upside down.

3. Cut or tear 1¼"-wide fabric strip; tie in a bow around candle holder.

4. Top with 3" candle.

Larger Candle Holders

1. Set 4" and 6" flowerpots upside down; top with upside-down 4" and 6" saucers.

2. Trim with torn or cut fabric strips, bows and/or buttons as desired; set 4" and 6" pillar candles on top.

Floral Centerpiece

1. Cut or tear 1¼"-wide fabric strip; tie in a bow around flowerpot.

2. Fill pot with floral foam trimmed to fit tightly.

3. Lay pot on side; fill with arrangement of berries, leaves and flowers.

Place Markers

1. *Each place marker:* Cut or tear two 6" fabric squares; glue together, wrong sides facing. Glue button in center on right side; place fabric in 2" flowerpot button up, arranging folds evenly. Fill pot with candies.

2. *Name tag:* Referring to Napkin Technique, apply motif to oven-shrink plastic sheet. While still wet, sprinkle lightly with fabric glitter; let dry and shake off excess.

3. Cut out design, adding a 1"–2" tab at bottom.

4. Write name on tag front using dimensional paint; let dry. Insert tab in pot.

Napkin Rings

1. *Each napkin ring:* Referring to Napkin Technique, apply motif to craft foam. While still wet, sprinkle lightly with fabric glitter; let dry and shake off excess.

2. Cut out design. Cut a vertical slit on each side of motif ¼" from edge.

3. Hold several strands of raffia together; thread through slits around fabric or paper napkin. Tie ends in bow on front of napkin ring.

Table Linens

1. *Centerpiece:* Tear 18" square of fabric to serve as background on which to arrange candles, floral arrangement, etc.

2. *Place mats:* Tear 18" x 12" rectangle fabric for each place mat. ✄

Winter Delights!

Winter brings many opportunities for creative expression as we craft one-of-a-kind gifts and decorations! This festive collection of wintry and Christmas crafts will give you dozens of ideas for making the yuletide season memorable for all your loved ones!

Snowflake photo by Patricia A. Rasmussen

Frosty Bottle Hugger

Next time you present a bottle of Christmas cheer, include this sweet and bubbly snowman crafted from cotton batting. Just insert the bottle into his arms.

Design by Mary Ayres

Materials

- Natural cotton batting*
- Woman's red knit sock
- Small piece orange felt
- 1" iridescent yellow pompom
- 2 (⅛") round black beads
- 3" x 22" torn strip of complementary fabric
- 2 (1") silk holly leaves with berries
- Black embroidery floss
- 2 cups doll pellets
- Polyester fiberfill
- Tacky craft glue
- Off-white thread
- Needles: hand-sewing and embroidery
- Pink powdered cosmetic blusher
- Cotton-tip swab

Warm and Natural needled cotton batting from The Warm Company.

Project Note

The side of the cotton batting with the brown specks is the wrong side. Sew all seams right sides facing, using ¼" seam allowance. Use tiny stitches and trim seams close to stitching.

Instructions

1. From batting cut two bodies, four arms and one base; cut also one 6" circle for head.

2. Sew arms together in pairs, leaving straight ends open. Trim seams and turn right side out; stuff closed ends lightly with fiberfill.

3. Pin straight ends of arms to sides of one body piece between dots, making sure tops of arms are on top. Baste arms to body. Lay remaining body over the first, sandwiching arms in between. Sew side seams, stitching through arms; trim seams.

4. Pin and sew base to bottom of body, matching dots on base with body side seams. Trim seams; turn body right side out. Tack ends of arms together with a few invisible stitches.

5. Baste around top of body close to edge. Pour doll pellets into bottom; stuff body lightly with fiberfill. Pull basting stitches tight to close top; knot.

6. *Head:* Baste around batting circle close to edge. Pull stitches tight to gather, leaving 1" opening; knot. Stuff head firmly and evenly with fiberfill. Pin gathered side of head

Continued on page 135

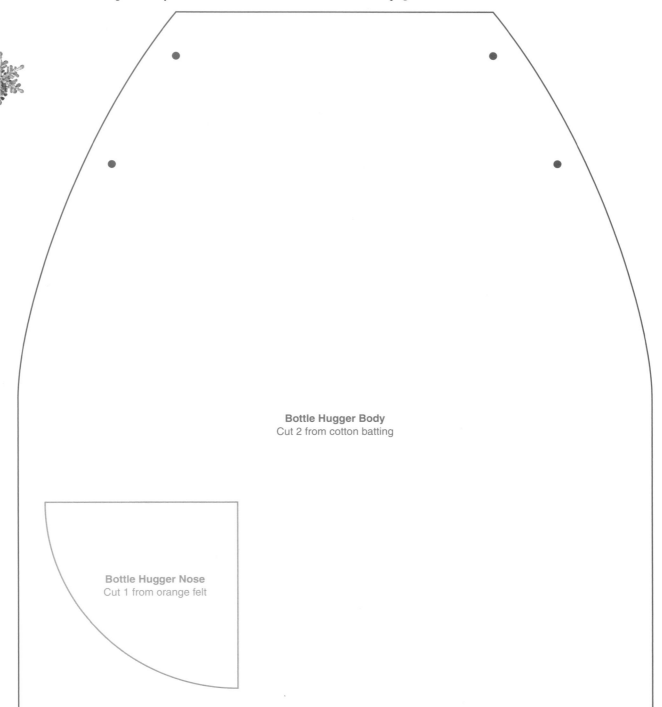

Bottle Hugger Body
Cut 2 from cotton batting

Bottle Hugger Nose
Cut 1 from orange felt

Santa Mini Tin

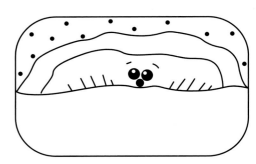

You're right—those little tin boxes are too nice to throw away!
Transform them into sweet little holiday holders for treats or tiny gifts.

Design by Paula Bales

Materials

- Mini 2⅜" x 1½" tin box from mint candies
- Wooden cutouts*: 2 small (⅝") eggs, 2 small (¾") holly leaves
- 3 (³⁄₁₆") jingle bells
- Metal paints*: bright white, real red, strawberry shake, true green
- Paintbrushes: #2 and #6 shaders
- Graphite transfer paper
- Stylus and toothpick
- Black fine-tip permanent marker
- Craft cement

Woodsies cutouts from Forster; No-Prep metal paints from DecoArt.

Instructions

1. Transfer pattern to tin's lid (refer to "Using Transfer and Graphite Paper" in the General Instructions, page 174).

2. Paint hat red; let dry. Apply random dots of green with toothpick. Paint face strawberry; let dry. Add red dot nose and lightly painted red cheeks. Paint hat fur and beard white. Let dry.

3. Paint eggs (mustache) white; paint holly leaves green and jingle bells red. Let dry.

4. Using black marker, outline hat brim, top of beard and mustache; add eyes and eyebrows. Outline leaves and draw veins down center. Using toothpick dipped in white, add highlight dot to each eye.

5. Glue mustache, leaves and jingle-bell berries to lid of tin.

6. Using toothpick, add random green dots and clusters of three red dots to side of tin's bottom. With black marker, add tiny dot to each green dot. ✄

Santa Mini Tin

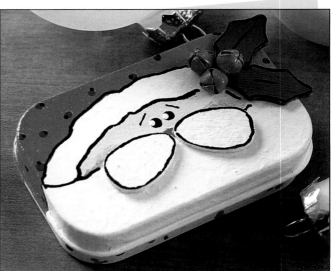

Fancy & Fun Frames

Get out your scraps and get ready for some freestyling creativity!

I discovered how much fun it was to make an abstract design on a frame when trying to figure out what to do with a ton of leather scraps. I cut the scraps into geometric shapes and glued them to the front and sides of an old frame. I was delighted with the results! By layering the scraps as I covered the frame, I created a very dimensional and tactile craft.

Stick to one type of scrap, like fabric, or mix it up with leftover glitter, buttons, charms, yarns and leather. Choose scraps of different shapes and sizes, but try to keep the sizes in proportion to the overall design if possible.

You'll need a sturdy photo frame (any type will do, from acrylic to wood). Feel free to recycle an old frame! Glue your scraps to the frame, building the design with depth and texture. It's best to use a thick tacky or jewelry glue so that the glue can bond light- and heavyweight scraps.

Fill in the entire frame surface (unless using an acrylic box frame; in that case, adhere scraps only to a small portion of the frame front and then the sides). Allow to dry completely before inserting photo or artwork. ✄

Cinnamon Stick Votive

Visit your grocery's bulk food section to purchase cinnamon sticks inexpensively for this sweet-smelling candle holder.

Design by Florence Bolen Tebbets

Materials

- Straight-sided glass votive candle holder, approximately 2" diameter with 3" sides
- Votive candle
- 20–25 3" cinnamon sticks
- 2 large rubber bands
- Tacky craft glue*
- Natural raffia
- Small sprig of red berries
- Craft pick

Crafters Pick Ultimate Tacky Glue from API.

Instructions

1. Place several cinnamon sticks side by side around outside of candle holder. Place one rubber band around top and one around bottom of candle holder to hold sticks in place. Continue adding cinnamon sticks, sliding them under rubber bands, until candle holder is covered.

2. Slide rubber bands to middle of cinnamon sticks; make sure both rubber bands lie flat.

3. Using craft pick, apply thick line of glue over rubber bands. Wrap raffia tightly around cinnamon sticks, covering glued rubber bands. Tie raffia ends in bow; glue red berries in center of bow. ✄

Flour Sifter Arrangement

An old sifter—or a cheap one from the discount store—
is the perfect "vase" for this fragrant, creative arrangement.

Design by Florence Bolen Tebbets

Materials

- 3-cup flour sifter
- 2 wooden spoons
- Floral foam
- Artificial evergreen sprigs
- Artificial red berry sprays
- Lacquered red apples: 7 large, 3–6 small
- 9–12 3" cinnamon sticks
- 3–5 whole nutmegs
- Wooden gingerbread cutouts: 2 (3"–4"), 4 (1½"–2")
- 1½ yards 1"-wide Christmasy plaid ribbon
- Brown acrylic paint
- Flat paintbrush
- Shiny white dimensional paint
- Craft picks
- Serrated knife
- Wire cutters
- Low-temperature glue gun
- Awl or ice pick
- Apple-cinnamon dried potpourri (optional)

Project Note

Apply a little glue to end of each pick before inserting it in foam.

Instructions

1. Paint gingerbread cutouts brown; let dry. Squeeze on faces and "icing" decorations with white paint; let dry.

2. With serrated knife, cut foam to fit snugly in bottom of sifter. Place a few small evergreen sprigs in bottom of sifter, adding some potpourri if desired; glue foam on top.

3. Cut evergreen in varying lengths; glue all around top of sifter to create base. Glue taller sprigs in

center of foam; glue in spoon handles. Add greenery to fill sifter.

4. Glue cinnamon sticks to ends of craft picks; pierce top of nutmegs with awl and glue ends of craft picks in holes. Glue apples, gingerbread, nutmegs and cinnamon sticks in arrangement, concealing craft picks in greenery. Add berries and small sprigs of greenery to fill any gaps.

5. Cut 9" from ribbon and cut chenille stem in half; set aside ribbon and one half of stem. Form remaining ribbon into three-loop bow; wrap center with half of chenille stem; glue in arrangement.

6. Fold remaining ribbon in half; wrap with chenille stem. Notch ribbon ends and glue in arrangement opposite larger bow. ✂

Frosty Bottle Hugger

Continued from page 131

to gathered top of body; sew together with invisible stitches.

7. *Nose:* Cut nose from orange felt; fold in half and sew straight edges together. Trim seam; turn right side out. Stuff with fiberfill; baste around open end of nose and pull tight to

gather; knot. Sew nose to center of face using invisible stitches. ***Note:*** *Center of face is directly above side seam on snowman's left side.*

8. *Face:* Lightly pencil 2" smile under nose. Using black floss, embroider mouth with stem stitch, hiding beginning and ending knots at bottom where they will be hidden by scarf. Sew eye beads ⅛" apart above nose, again hiding knots.

Rouge cheeks with cotton-tip swab and cosmetic blusher.

9. *Hat:* Cut 3" section from toe end of sock (toe seam is top of hat). Put sock on head and roll up edge for brim; glue. Glue pompom to top.

10. *Scarf:* Tie scarf around neck, knotting on left side. Insert holly in knot; spot-glue scarf and holly to snowman. ✂

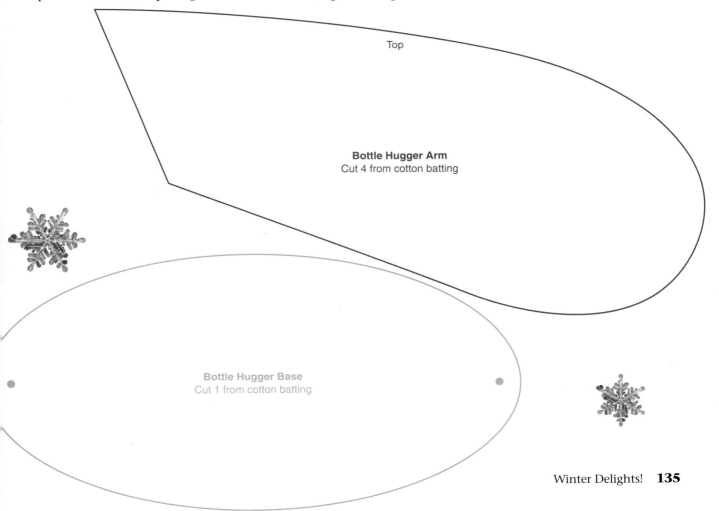

Top

Bottle Hugger Arm
Cut 4 from cotton batting

Bottle Hugger Base
Cut 1 from cotton batting

"Fleas Navidad!" Greeting Card

Have fun stamping whimsical designs to make a distinctive holiday card for every dog lover on your list!

Design by Vicki Blizzard

Materials

- Stamps*: dogs and Christmas designs
- Card stock: topaz parchment, Christmas red, white
- Mask
- Adhesive-backed foam spacer dots
- Pigment stamp pads*: brown, evergreen
- Clear sparkle liquid glitter*
- Glue*
- Paper glaze*
- Brush-tip markers*: fawn, pure red, spring green
- Writer markers*: hunter green, pure black, pure red
- 8" ¼"-wide evergreen feather-edge ribbon
- Paper crimper

Clear Impressions dogs set #35-9351 and Christmas set #35-9388 stamps from Provo Craft; Color Box Cat's Eye stamp pads and Star Writer liquid glitter from Clearsnap Inc.; 2-in-1 Glue and paper glaze from Aleene's; Scroll & Brush Markers #MS5000 and Writer markers #MS-6600 from EK Success Ltd.

Instructions

1. *Card base:* Cut 5" x 4¾" red card stock and 3¾" square topaz card stock; run topaz through crimper. Glue in center of red card stock leaving even ⅜" border. Tie ribbon in bow; trim ends. Glue bow to center top of red card stock.

2. *Pocket:* Cut 4⅝" x 1⅞" topaz card stock. Glue bottom and sides to bottom of card base, leaving ⅛" margin around bottom and sides. Cut 4¼" x 1½" red card stock; glue to topaz pocket.

3. Ink garland stamp with evergreen ink; stamp image on white card stock. Using .5mm end of red writer marker, dot berries throughout garland. Let dry.

4. Rub thin layer of liquid glitter over garland image. When dry, dot each berry with a small dot of paper glaze to form dimensional berries. Let dry, then trim around garland close to stamped image.

5. Stamp three bones on white card stock; color with brush end of fawn marker, coating edges with second and third layers for shading. When dry, apply two or three coats paper glaze, allowing each to dry thoroughly. Cut out bones. Glue bones to garland.

6. *Card insert:* Fold in half 2¾" x 5½" piece red card stock to make 2¾" square card; position fold at top. Cut 2¼" square topaz card stock; glue to center front of card.

7. Ink bow stamp with evergreen ink; stamp image on white card stock and mask. When ink dries, cut out mask and place on top of image on card stock.

8. Using evergreen ink, stamp evergreen frame on top of masked bow, centering bow at bottom of frame. Stamp a second frame on another

Continued on page 139

Snowman & Santa Cards

Rub-on transfers and paper punches make it easy to create lots of beautiful cards quickly!

Designs by Bev George

Materials

Set of Four Cards

- 4 A7 card blanks (7" x 10" card stock) with matching envelopes*
- Rub-on transfers*: Christmas images and Christmas messages
- Paper punches*: 2 snowflakes, star

- 4 pieces assorted card stock* cut 4½" x 6½": green, red, two white
- Deckle paper edgers
- Glue
- Permanent fine-tip markers: red, black
- Holiday stencil*

*Card blanks from Paper Reflections; First Impressions Rub-On Transfers "Three Cheers for Christmas" #41-8108 and "Share the Cheer" #41-8660 from Provo Craft; Christmas 6-in-1 Craft Punch by HyGlo; snowflake and star punches from EK Success Ltd.; Mat Stacks card stock from View Enterprise; Holiday/Special Occasions stencil from Deja Views.

Continued on page 139

Holiday Totes

Cut down your wrapping time and clean out that drawer of
scrapbooking leftovers to create your own imaginative gift bags!

Designs by Leslie Frederick

Holiday Elf

Materials
- 8" x 10¼" kraft paper bag
- Die-cut elf*
- Paper gift and plaid corner accents*
- 8½" x 11" sheets red and green paper
- Glue
- Red and green raffia

My Mind's Eye Die-Cut Friend in Santa's Bag and Corner Accents— Gifts and Plaid from Frame It Up.

Instructions
1. Cut green paper 7½" x 8½" and red paper 5½" x 6"; glue to bag.

2. Glue elf in center; add corner accents.

3. Add bow tied from red and green raffia.

Friends & Mittens

Materials
- 8" x 10¼" kraft paper bag
- Pad of Christmasy paper scraps*
- Red heart-shaped novelty button
- Jute or twine
- Glue stick
- Decorative paper edgers (optional)

"It's Christmas" Bitty Scrap Pad from Provo Craft.

Instructions
1. Cut or tear 2⅜" x 4" rectangles from snowman plaid and green paper on scrap pad; adhere to bag.

2. Using snowman print with words and mitten border, tear or cut red and gold mittens into 1¼" x 1¾" rectangles. Tear 1¾" x 2½" rectangle from snowman plaid; adhere to center of bag.

3. Carefully tear around snowman, words and green mittens. Add small piece of jute to mittens and adhere with button to bottom middle rectangle.

4. Adhere words and snowman as shown. Add jute bow to bag. ✄

"Fleas Navidad!" Greeting Card

Continued from page 136

piece of white card stock. Using .5mm end of red writer marker, dot berries on evergreen frame. Let dry.

9. Rub thin layer of liquid glitter over one frame image. When dry, dot each berry with a small dot of paper glaze. Let dry, then trim around both images outside stamped area. Glue unglittered frame inside card.

10. Using brown ink, stamp Chihuahua on topaz card stock; color inside ears and feet with fawn brush marker. Color collar red; color tag spring green; color eyes and nose black. Apply paper glaze to collar, tag, nose and eyes; let dry. Trim image close to stamped outline. Apply foam dots to back of image; apply to center of frame on card front.

11. Using .5mm hunter green writer marker, write "Fleas Navidad!" on inside frame; add dots and swirls to letters. Place card in pocket on card base. ✄

Snowman & Santa Cards

Continued from page 137

"Share the Cheer!"
1. Trim ⅜" off long edge of card front using paper edgers.

2. Apply rub-on border along long edge of card back so that it is visible from front.

3. Trim all four sides of green card stock with deckle edgers; glue inside card.

4. Apply rub-on transfers: snowman, stars, "Share the Cheer!" and holly to card front, and section of border to top of insert.

"Happy Holidays"
1. Trim long edge of card front using paper edgers.

2. Trim all four sides of red card stock with deckle edgers; glue inside card.

3. Using pencil, lightly trace "Happy Holidays" from stencil on card front; retrace with permanent markers.

4. Apply rub-on transfers: snowman, Santa, mini hearts and trees to card front, and inner borders to insert.

"I Love Snowy Days"
1. Using two different snowflake punches, punch five snowflakes along long edge of card front and one in lower left corner; reserve snowflakes.

2. Punch snowflake pattern down left (long) edge of white card stock; reserve snowflakes. Glue card stock inside card.

3. Glue punched snowflakes from insert sheet to front cover; glue snowflakes from cover inside insert sheet.

4. Apply rub-on transfers: snowman, holly on collar, sayings on front and sayings inside.

"May All Your Christmases Be Bright"
1. Punch six stars along opening edge of front cover; reserve stars.

2. Punch seven stars on left (long) edge of white card stock, punching a few stars off the edge; reserve stars. Glue card stock inside card.

3. Apply rub-on transfers of Santa, saying and stars to cover.

Envelopes
Decorate envelopes with matching rub-ons and remaining punched motifs from cards and card stock. ✄

Country Canvas Holiday Pins

Rich, old-fashioned colors give these quick-and-easy pins the warmth of Christmases past.

Designs by Deborah Spofford

Country Canvas Holidays Pins

Materials

All Six Pins

- 10" round canvas clock face or place mat*
- Acrylic paints*: antique gold, barn red, dark forest green, nightfall blue, timberline green
- Paintbrushes: #1, #2 and #10 shaders, #1 round, #2/0 detail
- Transfer paper and stylus
- Mahogany gel wood stain*
- Lint-free cloth
- Black fine-point permanent marker
- Water-based matte varnish*
- 6 (1") pin backs
- Tacky glue or hot-glue gun

*Kreative Kanvas from Kunin; Ceramcoat acrylic paints, Home Décor gel wood stain and Ceramcoat varnish, all from Delta.

Instructions

1. Cut one of each shape from canvas.

2. Using #10 shader, base-coat shapes, referring to "Painting Techniques" in the General Instructions, page 174: *heart*—blue; *tree*—green; *star*—gold; *mitten*—green on cuff and red on remainder; *hand*—gold; *cottage*—blue on roof and red on remainder. Let dry.

3. Lightly transfer details to each pin, using transfer paper and referring to "Using Transfer and Graphite Paper" in the General Instructions, page 174.

4. Add painted details, then let dry completely:

Heart—Paint one red patch and one gold patch, slightly overlapping.

Tree—Paint one red patch and one gold patch, slightly overlapping.

Using #2/0 detail brush, line gold "stars" on remainder of tree.

Star—Paint blue heart in center.

Mitten—Paint gold heart on mitten. Using stylus dipped in blue, dot clusters of three dots over red portion of mitten.

Hand— Paint red heart in center.

Cottage—Using #2 shader, paint cottage windows gold. Using #1 round brush and green, paint cottage door and heart on roof. Dot on doorknob with stylus dipped in blue.

5. Using lint-free cloth, apply gel stain to each pin. Wipe off excess

stain and let pins dry.

6. Using fine-point pen, add details to tree, heart and cottage:

Heart—Add a few "stitches" over edges of patches; add simulated "blanket stitches" around edges.

Tree—Add a few "stitches" over edges of patches.

Cottage—Outline and draw panes in windows; define line between roof and rest of cottage; add accent marks on each side of heart.

7. Paint each pin with matte varnish; let dry.

8. Glue pin backs to pins. ✁

Snazzy Snowmen Runner

Chilly snowmen in hot colors brighten wintry days
on this colorful runner for your table or buffet.

Design by Leslie Hartsock

Materials

- Fabrics: ½ yard fuchsia with gold swirls, ⅓ yard dark blue print, ⅛ yard yellow print, ¼ yard white-on-white print, ⅛ yard sky blue print, scraps of orange print and pink polka-dot fabrics, ½ yard backing fabric
- 9" x 12" felt sheets*: pink mist, misty blue, spring yellow
- 1¼ yards fusible paper web*
- ¾ yard tear-away stabilizer*
- ½ yard quilt fleece
- Buttons: 3 (¾") orange flat, 6 (⅛") black flat
- Rayon threads* to match fabrics
- Clear monofilament thread
- All-purpose sewing threads: black, white, orange
- Quilt basting spray*
- Rotary cutter and mat
- Sewing machine with zigzag and even-feed "walking" foot
- Straight pins
- Hand-sewing needle
- Iron
- Pressing cloth

Kunin felts Rainbow Classic and Flashfelt; Pellon Wonder-Under fusible web and Stitch-n-Tear stabilizer; Sulky rayon threads; Sullivan's Quilt Basting Spray.

Cutting

1. Using rotary cutter and mat, cut three 9½" x 10½" background panels from dark blue fabric.

2. Cut five 2½"-wide strips across width of fuchsia fabric; cut those into six 9½" pieces and four 10½" strips; reserve remaining strips for binding.

3. From yellow fabric cut eight 2½" squares.

Snowman Panels

1. Trace three sets of all pattern pieces (page 144) on paper side of fusible web, tracing pattern components individually and leaving space between each; cut apart.

2. Following manufacturer's instructions and referring to photo, fuse patterns for snowmen and hats to wrong sides of fabrics. Using pressing cloth fuse scarves to pink, blue and yellow felts.

3. Cut out pieces; remove backing. Arrange appliqués on blue panels, aligning bottom of snowmen with fabric edge and leaving at least ½"

seam allowance at top. Fuse using pressing cloth.

4. Pin stabilizer behind areas to be appliquéd. Mark appliqué lines on ends of scarves to correspond with dotted lines on pattern; scarf ends will be left free and fringed as shown.

5. Using matching rayon threads in top of machine and white all-purpose thread in bobbin, satin-stitch around appliqués, beginning with pieces that are behind others. Clip threads, tear away stabilizer and fringe ends of scarves.

Assembly

1. Using ¼" seam allowance and matching threads throughout, sew 9½" fuchsia strips to top and bottom of panels; press seams.

2. Sew yellow squares to ends of 10½" strips; press seams. Pin between panels and at ends of runner. Sew; press seams.

3. Using a sweeping motion, spray basting spray on wrong side of runner and backing fabric; let dry. Sandwich batting between top and backing.

4. Thread top of machine with monofilament and bobbin with white thread; fit with walking foot. Machine-quilt around center snowman, then in ditch of block. Repeat on other blocks.

5. *Binding:* Sew remaining fuchsia strips together to make one long strip. Press in half, wrong sides facing. With edges even and right sides facing, sew strip to front of runner, mitering corners.

6. Trim excess fleece, backing fabric and binding. Turn binding to back of quilt; turn under raw edges and hand-stitch.

7. Sew black button eyes and orange buttons to snowmen. ✂

Sew

Cut

Snazzy Snowmen Runner

Cookies Gift Bag

Simple brown lunch bags become distinctive wraps for your homemade treats with the simple addition of a few fabric scraps.

Design by Florence Bolen Tebbets

Materials

- Brown paper lunch bag
- Double-sided adhesive sheet*
- ¼ yard gingerbread cookies fabric*
- Pinking shears for fabric
- Pinking paper edgers*
- Paper punch (optional)

PeelnStick double-sided adhesive from Therm O Web; VIP Gingerbread Cookies fabric; Fiskars paper edgers.

Project Note

The ¼ yard fabric will enable you to make many gift bags with many variations.

Instructions

1. Referring to photo, locate area of fabric with "Grandma's Gingerbread" recipe and other motifs. Peel backing from one side of adhesive sheet; press onto fabric. Using pinking shears throughout, cut out desired motifs.

2. From *unbacked* area of fabric, cut 1" x 24" strip for tie.

3. Lay bag flat with seam on back. Fold top down to front 1½".

4. Punch two holes about 2" apart through all layers of bag about ½" below fold.

5. Peel backing from fabric motifs; apply to front of bag. Using paper edgers, round off edge.

6. Place goodies inside bag; close, again folding down top to front. Thread fabric strip through holes and tie shut with bow on front of bag. ✂

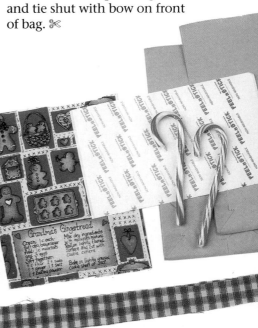

"I Love Snow" Wall Hanging

Looking up into a starry midwinter sky, this happy snowman will help you celebrate the season's joys.

Design by Chris Malone

Materials

- Fabrics: 10" x 11" black solid, ⅛ yard red-and-black print, ¾ yard woven black-and-white check, 4" x 6" white solid, 2" x 5" woven red-and-black check, and small pieces of orange solid and brown-and-tan check
- White graphite paper
- 6-strand embroidery floss: white, black
- Embroidery needle and hoop
- Extra-strength iron-on adhesive
- Low-loft batting
- Quilting needle and quilting threads: red, black (optional)
- Pink powdered cosmetic blusher
- 2 (3mm) black beads
- ½" x ⅞" primitive-style heart button
- Red acrylic craft paint
- Small paintbrush
- 7 (⅜₆") flat white buttons
- Seam sealant
- 2 plastic bone rings

Project Notes

All piecing is done with fabric right sides together. All seams are ¼".

Border strips are cut long and trimmed later to allow for individual differences in piecing.

Assembly and quilting can be done by hand or machine.

All embroidery is done with 2 strands floss.

Snowman Panel

1. Centering pattern (page 148) on black solid fabric, transfer patterns for ground line and lettering using graphite paper (refer to "Using Transfer and Graphite Paper" in the General Instructions, page 174).

2. Secure fabric in hoop. Backstitch lettering with white floss, adding French knots at ends and intersections of lines. Mark ground line with outline or stem stitch.

3. Apply iron-on adhesive to wrong sides of white, orange and brown-and-tan check fabrics, and to 2" x 1" piece of red-and-black check fabric. Cut snowman from white, scarf front from red-and-black check, nose from orange and twig arms from brown-and-tan check.

4. Peel backing from each appliqué; position on fabric, overlapping where indicated by dashed lines. Fuse in place.

5. Using fingertip, apply blusher to cheeks. Backstitch smile with black floss, adding French knots at ends; add French knot eyes.

Piecing & Assembly

1. Trim ½" from each side of snowman panel so that it measures 9" x 10".

2. Cut 1" x 44" border strip from red-and-black print; sew to top of snowman panel; trim ends even. Repeat across bottom of panel, then down sides.

3. Cut two 2½" x 44" frame strips from black-and-white check; reserve remaining black-and-white fabric for backing. Using same method as step 2, sew frame strips to red-and-black border strips across top, bottom and down sides. Press all seams outward.

4. Place batting on flat surface; smooth out any bumps. Smooth backing fabric right side up on top of batting. Lay snowman panel right side down on backing fabric.

5. Pin all three layers together to secure. Trim batting and backing even with snowman panel. Using quilting thread, sew around all edges, leaving 5" opening at center bottom for turning. Trim batting close to seam and trim corners. Turn right side out; press. Fold under seam allowance around opening and stitch by hand to close.

6. Pin or baste through centers of border and frame strips to hold layers in place for quilting. Using matching quilting thread and sewing by hand or machine, stitch "in the ditch" (as close to seam as possible) between snowman panel and red-and-black border strips and between border and frame strips.

Finishing

1. Paint heart button red. Let dry. Sew to snowman's body with red quilting thread. Using black, sew bead eyes in place.

2. Cut ¾" x 5" strip from red-and-black checked fabric; apply seam sealant along long edges and let dry. Fringe short ends ½". Tie knot in center of strip; tack to scarf front with needle and thread.

3. Sew white buttons to background for snowflakes using white floss.

4. Sew plastic hanging rings on wrong side of wall hanging at top corners. ✄

Pattern on page 148

Ho Ho Ho

Orange

Brown-and-Tan Check

Black-and-Red Check

White

I Love Snow

"I Love Snow" Wall Hanging

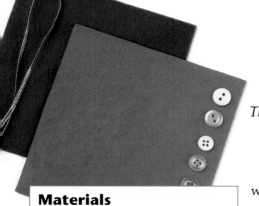

Buttoned Stars

These little stars are a scrap crafter's delight, swallowing up remnants of felt and excess buttons, with only a few simple, long stitches!

Designs by Helen L. Rafson

Materials

Each Ornament

- Felt*: red, pirate green
- Cotton embroidery floss: red, green, yellow-orange
- Embroidery needle
- Assorted small white flat buttons
- Polyester fiberfill
- 9" ⅛"-wide gold ribbon
- Tacky craft glue
- Pinking shears

*Kunin felt.

Instructions

1. Using scissors, cut two large stars from red or green felt and one small star from other color.

2. Arrange buttons on small star; secure with dots of glue, then stitch in place with all 6 strands red or green floss, using color to match larger stars.

3. Glue button star to one larger star; let dry.

4. Using all 6 strands yellow-orange floss, outline button star with 10 long, straight stitches.

5. Glue a little stuffing in center of remaining large star; glue large stars together along edges. Let dry; trim edges with pinking shears.

6. *Hanger:* Fold gold ribbon in half; glue ends to back of star. ✄

Large Star
Cut 2 from red or green

Small Star
Cut 1 from red or green

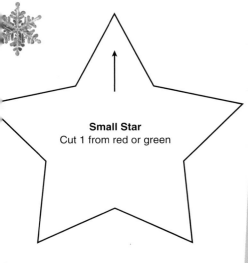

Peek-a-Boo Party Pockets

Created from mini boxes and craft-foam scraps, these sweet pets are ideal party favors and holders for tiny treasures.

Designs by Lorine Mason

Materials

Set of Three

- Mini tree and 2 mini star boxes
- Acrylic craft paints*: cadmium yellow, mistletoe, true red
- Sparkle varnish
- Craft foam scraps: white, black, green, pink
- 5mm pompoms: 3 pink, 9 red
- 2 (5mm) wiggly eyes
- Paint pens: fine-point black, metallic gold
- Glue
- Paintbrush
- Fine sandpaper

Americana acrylic paints from DecoArt.

Instructions

1. Sand edges of boxes lightly.

2. Paint all surfaces of boxes as shown, adding second coat if necessary. Let dry.

3. Paint boxes with sparkle varnish, adding a second coat if desired. Let dry.

4. *Cut pieces from craft foam:* Cut one kitty head and tail each from black and white; cut tail tip, muzzle and inner ear from white; cut puppy head, ears, three kitty paws and two puppy paws from white and one kitty paw from black; cut six leaves from green.

5. Using black pen, add eyes, noses and other details to foam pieces as shown. (Note that black kitty will have wiggly eyes and pink pompom nose.)

6. Referring to photo, glue ears to back of puppy head; glue white tail tip to black kitty's tail, inner ear to her left ear, and muzzle to her face. Glue a pair of green leaves and three red pompoms to each head. Flatten two pink pompoms for cheeks and glue to white kitty; glue remaining pink pompom to black kitty for nose.

7. Glue all heads and tails behind front edge of boxes. Glue paws to fronts of boxes.

8. Use gold pen to personalize boxes or outline with gold dots, etc. ✄

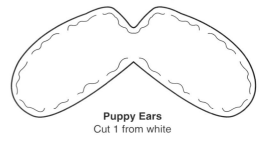

Puppy Ears
Cut 1 from white

Puppy Paw
Cut 2 from white

Puppy Head
Cut 1 from white

Holly
Cut 6 from green

Kitty Head
Cut 1 from black and 1 from white

Kitty Paw
Cut 3 from white and 1 from black

Tail Tip
Cut 1 from white

Inner Ear
Cut 1 from white

Tail
Cut 1 from black and 1 from white

Muzzle
Cut 1 from white

Santa Oil Lamp

*The addition of a wick and glass tube transforms
a painted mayo jar into a work of holiday
art worthy of anyone on your gift list!*

Design by Mary Ayres

Santa Oil Lamp

Materials

- Oil lamp wick with glass tube*
- Recycled glass pint jar with metal lid
- 10" ⅜"-wide white satiny braid or trim
- Artificial holly leaves with berries
- ⅜ yard ⅜"-wide wire-edge silver ribbon
- ¾" round wooden head plug
- Glass paints*: baby pink, gloss black, gloss white, medium flesh
- Real red metal paint*
- Paintbrushes: #6 round, #5 and #8 natural bristle
- Silver extra-fine-tip opaque writer*
- Craft glue*
- Graphite or transfer paper
- Stylus
- Vinegar
- Craft drill with ⅜" bit
- Scrap wood block
- Rubber mallet
- Lamp oil

Lamp wick from Craft Catalog; Ultra Gloss AirDry Enamel glass paints and No-Prep Metal Paint from DecoArt; ZIG Memory System writer from EK Success Ltd.; Kids Choice Glue from Beacon.

Project Note

Apply three or four coats paint on glass and metal surfaces, allowing paint to dry between coats, for opaque coverage. Apply paints in pouncing or dabbing motion with round bristle brush for even coverage.

Instructions

1. Wash jar with soap and water; remove all traces of adhesive and label. Moisten paper towel with vinegar; wipe clean jar and lid; let dry. Take care not to touch areas that will be painted.

2. Hold jar by placing fingers *inside*. Paint entire outside of jar white. Let dry. Transfer face and mustache details to jar (top of head should be even with bottom edge of jar lip), referring to directions for "Using Transfer and Graphite Paper" in the General Instructions, page 174.

3. Paint face and wooden plug flesh; paint cheeks and ⅜" circle in center of plug pink. Using large brush handle dipped in black, dot on eyes. Using small brush handle, dot white highlights on eyes, cheeks and nose. Let dry.

4. Dot outline around face, cheeks, mustache and nose with silver writer. Let dry.

5. Place jar lid on scrap wood block and drill hole in center. Flatten rough edges with mallet.

6. Paint lid red; let dry.

7. Screw lid onto jar. Glue nose at top of mustache. Glue braid trim around top of jar, overlapping in back. Glue holly to lid; tie ribbon in bow and trim ends; glue to lid over greenery. Let dry.

8. Insert glass tube and wick in hole in lid. Fill jar with lamp oil. ✄

Gingerbread Switch-Plate Cover

This candy cane and gingerbread switch cover looks almost good enough to eat.
Replace your everyday switch covers with this festive alternative.

Design by Shelia Sommers

Materials

- Ceramic switch-plate cover*
- Surface conditioner*
- Clear gloss glaze*
- Thinner dilutant*
- Enamel paints*: chili pepper red, chocolate, cotton candy pink, dark goldenrod, ultra black, ultra white
- Paintbrushes: #6 and #20 flats, ¼" angular, 10/0 liner
- Metallic silver run-on snowflake transfers*
- White graphite paper
- Stylus
- Tracing paper

Switch-plate cover from American Art Clay; PermEnamel conditioner, glaze, thinner dilutant and paints, and Renaissance Foil Gilded Accents snowflakes transfers, all from Delta.

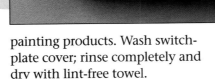

Instructions

1. Carefully read manufacturer's instructions for using paints and painting products. Wash switch-plate cover; rinse completely and dry with lint-free towel.

2. Apply surface conditioner to front and sides of switch-plate cover; let air dry.

3. Paint center of cover black up to lip at edges. Let dry for several hours, then apply a second coat. Let dry.

4. Paint red peppermint stripe pattern on edge using #6 flat brush for wide stripes and liner for narrow stripes. Let dry completely.

5. Referring to "Using Transfer & Graphite Paper" in the General Instructions, page 174, transfer pattern for gingerbread man to switch-plate cover with white graphite paper.

6. Referring to "Painting Techniques" in the General Instructions, page 174, paint gingerbread man dark goldenrod; shade with chocolate. Paint eyes black. Thin pink with dilutant and add cheeks. Thin black; add mouth and eyelashes using liner. Float on chocolate nose. Using liner, add wavy white line around each section of gingerbread man. Let dry completely.

7. Referring to manufacturer's instructions, apply snowflakes randomly to switch-plate cover.

8. Coat front and sides of switch-plate cover with clear gloss glaze; let dry completely. ✂

Gingerbread Man

Happy Thumbprint Jars

*Start with a thumbprint and some recycled jars—and end up
with a trio of colorful containers for your favorite snacks and treats.*

Designs by Annie Lang

Materials

- Glass jars with lids: 1-quart, plus large and small baby-food jars
- Coordinating fabric scraps
- 1"-wide white ruffled lace
- Ribbon bows
- Fiberfill
- Craft glue or hot-glue gun
- Glossy paints*: gloss white, gloss black, cadmium yellow, Christmas red, Christmas green, hunter, baby blue, true blue
- Paintbrushes: #2 and #5 pointed rounds, size 2/0 liner
- Stylus
- Rubbing alcohol
- Corner cut from household sponge
- Palette
- Water container
- Tracing paper and pencil

UltraGloss paints from DecoArt.

Preparation

1. Trace character detail patterns onto tracing paper. Flip paper over; retrace lines with pencil. Flip paper back over to original side.

2. Remove labels and residue from jars with hot soapy water; dry. Wipe outside of jar with alcohol and water to remove any oils from fingers.

Base-Coating

Using corner cut from sponge, base-coat each jar with two coats paint, allowing adequate drying time between coats and following instructions for individual designs. Tap sponge up and down on palette a few times to work paint into sponge. Gently tap color onto glass using a pouncing motion.

Snowman Jar: Working on 1-quart jar, apply 3"-wide band of true blue around center. Turn jar upside down. Starting at bottom edge of true blue, paint bottom of jar baby blue. Let dry. Using #5 round brush, "squiggle" a white border along top and bottom edges of true blue.

Penguin Jar: Working with a large baby-food jar, paint ¾" line of hunter around jar about 1" below top. Paint 1½" band of baby blue just under hunter. Turn jar upside down. Starting at bottom of blue, paint bottom of jar hunter. Let dry. Using #5 round brush, "squiggle" a white border along top edge of hunter band and along top and bottom edges of true blue.

Snowflake Jar: Working with a small baby-food jar, paint sides and bottom of jar baby blue beginning about ½" from top. Let dry. Using #5 round brush, "squiggle" a white border along top edge of baby blue.

Thumbprint Characters

Characters are randomly painted around jars. After each thumbprint is dry, add details by placing traced design over the area and retracing with a stylus. To create thumbprint, dip thumb into white paint, then gently press onto palette a few times to evenly distribute paint. Gently press thumb onto jar.

Snowman

1. Two overlapping prints create head and tummy. For body, turn thumb upside down and gently press white thumbprint onto true blue background. With thumb right side up, press another print just above body for head.

Snowman Jar

Penguin Jar

Snowflake Jar

2. Use #2 round brush to add small red nose. Tap red onto cheeks; add black twiggy arms. Use #5 brush to add green or red scarf and ear-muffs. Using liner and black, add eyes, smile, earmuff and scarf out-lines. Using liner, add white move-ment lines and springy looped lines below snowman.

3. Fill in around snowmen with clusters of white, red and green dots, using stylus. Add white letter-ing with #2 round brush.

Penguin

1. Stamp white thumbprints around

center of blue band. When dry, use #5 round brush to outline each with black, creating a penguin. Use three strokes of black to make each wing on opposite sides of body.

2. Add yellow feet and beaks. Tap red onto cheeks. Outline and add black facial details and two "motion" lines at wings and feet using liner.

3. Using stylus, add green dots on hunter background.

Snowflakes

1. Randomly place large and small white thumbprints around jar. Pull eight small white lines out from edges of each large snowflake. Add white dot to end of each line to create large snowflake. Paint eight white dots around edges of smaller snowflakes.

2. Add red nose; tap color onto cheeks. Using liner, add black eyes, smiles and movement lines.

Lids

1. Glue small mound of fiberfill on center of each jar lid.

2. Cut 5" fabric circle for quart jar and 4" circle for baby-food jars. Center fabric over fiberfill; gather and glue edges to sides of lid. Screw lid onto jar.

3. Cut 10" lace for quart jar lid and 7" for baby-food jar lids. Glue around edge of lid. Glue ribbon bow to lace. ✄

Sweet Shop Tissue Topper

Iridescent glitter frosts this sweet topper created with wooden cutouts and colorful paints.

Design by Mary Ayres

Materials

- Tissue box cover*
- 12 wooden craft sticks*
- Wooden cutouts*: 5 (¾" x 1½") rectangles, 1" x 2" rectangle, 2 (1½") squares, 7 (¾") hearts, 6 (¾") trees, 2 (1¼") trees, 2 (1¾") candy canes
- Ultra-fine iridescent glitter
- Acrylic craft paints*: bright green, lavender, primary yellow, spice pink, true red, white wash
- #5 and #8 natural bristle paintbrushes
- Craft glue*
- Permanent markers*: fine-tip black, bullet-tip red
- Extra-fine-tip opaque white permanent writer*
- Boutique-style box of tissues

Pop Up tissue box cover from Beck Hill Group; craft sticks and Woodsies cutouts from Forster; Americana acrylic paints from DecoArt; Kids Choice Glue from Beacon; ZIG Memory System markers and writer from EK Success Ltd.

Instructions

1. Paint sides of tissue box pink; paint top white. Let dry, then dot pink over white top with paintbrush handle.

2. Paint one ¾" x 1½" rectangle (sign) and two squares (windows) yellow. Paint four ¾" x 1½" rectangles (shutters) and 1" x 2" rectangle (door) lavender. Paint hearts red; paint trees green; paint craft sticks and candy canes white. Let dry.

3. Add rounded candy-cane stripes to craft sticks and candy canes with red marker, reversing one candy cane. Using black marker, write "SWEET SHOP" on sign and add outline; divide each window into 16 equal panes. Using white writer, outline hearts with dots. Let dry.

Bitty Bulb Tote

*Raid your collection of scrapbooking leftovers and embellish
a ready-made cardboard tote to make this one-of-a-kind gift box.*

Design by Leslie Frederick

Materials

- Small red cardboard gift tote*
- Pad of Christmasy paper scraps*
- Christmas tree light stickers*
- Yellow-and-white gingham paper sticker border*
- Craft wire

Highsmith Corruboard small gift bag; "It's Christmas" Bitty Scrap Pad and Bitty Stickers tree light stickers from Provo Craft; Me and My Big Ideas Sticker Border.

Instructions

1. Assemble box according to manufacturer's instructions.

2. Add gingham border stickers along on top and bottom edges.

3. Cut out light bulbs; adhere one framed set of light bulbs to each side of box.

4. Coil wire; entwine it around handles, accenting it with light-bulb stickers, sandwiching wire between stickers of the same color. ✂

Sweet Shop Tissue Topper

4. Dilute glue with a little water. One piece at a time, paint entire top surfaces of shutters, door, trees, craft sticks and candy canes with mixture and immediately sprinkle with glitter. Dot

glue in center of each heart with brush handle; immediately sprinkle with glitter. Brush glue around edges of sign and windows; immediately sprinkle with glitter. When dry, shake off excess glitter.

5. Insert boutique-style box of tissues in cover. Glue craft sticks

around edges on front and sides (back is left plain).

6. Glue door, candy canes and trees to front; glue heart to door. Glue sign and hearts above door.

7. On both sides, glue window and shutters; glue hearts to shutters. Glue one large and two small trees at bottom. Let dry. ✂

Penguin Card Holder

His bright colors make this hardworking penguin a welcome guest on the mantel, counter, anywhere you want to display holiday greetings. He's a super note minder, too!

Design by Mary Ayres

Materials

- 14" wooden picket*
- 2 (2") wood blocks*
- Mini craft stick*
- Wooden craft spoon*
- 6 mini spring clothespins*
- Wooden cutouts*: 4 (⅞") stars, 3 (1¼") stars, ¾" circle, 2 (⅜") circles, 1" triangle, 1½" oval
- Acrylic craft paints*: bright green, lamp black, lavender, primary yellow, pumpkin, royal fuchsia, sapphire, white wash
- Paintbrushes: #6 round, #5 and #8 natural bristle
- Black twin-tip permanent marker*
- Craft glue*
- Fine sandpaper
- Graphite or transfer paper
- Stylus

Picket from J.B. Wood Products; blocks from Lara's Crafts; craft stick, spoon, clothespins and Woodsies cutouts from Forster; Americana paints from DecoArt; ZIG Memory System marker from EK Success Ltd.; Kids Choice Glue from Beacon.

Instructions

1. Sand wooden pieces as needed.

2. Referring to pattern and directions for "Using Transfer and Graphite Paper" in the General Instructions, page 174, transfer outside line around face onto picket, extending lines to bottom; transfer dashed hat line onto picket.

3. Paint picket white inside line; paint lavender above dashed line. Paint blocks, clothespins and remainder of picket black. Let dry.

4. Paint stars yellow, mini craft stick green for hat brim, triangle pumpkin for nose, and ⅜" circles fuchsia for cheeks; paint remaining pieces—spoon, oval and ¾" circle—blue for scarf. Let dry.

5. Using paintbrush handle dipped in paint, dot lavender hat with fuchsia and blue pieces with green; let dry. Add single white highlight in center of each cheek; let dry.

6. Using marker's bullet tip, add eyes. Using fine tip, outline stars, brim, hat, scarf pieces, cheeks, nose and white area.

Add nostrils to nose and fringe to ends of scarf oval and spoon.

7. For scarf, glue blue oval atop spoon and blue circle atop oval; glue scarf to penguin. Glue on cheeks, nose, hat brim and small star to hat.

8. Glue remaining stars to clothespins; glue flat surfaces of clothespins to sides of penguin, alternating small and large stars.

9. Glue one block atop the other; stand penguin and glue blocks to back at bottom; let dry. ✂

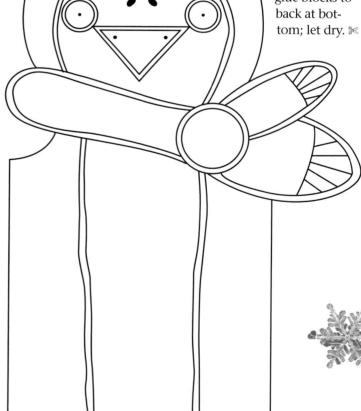

Penguin Card Holder

Clothespin Santa

Hang him from your tree or stand him on your knickknack shelf—
this little Santa is fun to paint and display!

Design by Dorothy Egan

Materials

- Acrylic craft paints*: base flesh, burgundy wine, lamp black, Santa red, titanium white
- Paintbrushes: #2 and #6 synthetic flat, #1 synthetic liner
- Wooden doll pin*
- Wooden doll pin stand* (optional)
- Fine cord (optional)
- Antiquing glaze
- Satin-finish varnish
- Stylus or toothpick
- Transfer paper
- Sandpaper
- Soft cloth

Americana acrylic paints from DecoArt; doll pin and stand from Forster.

Instructions

1. Sand doll pin (and stand) as needed. Transfer design to clothespin (refer to "Using Transfer and Graphite Paper" in the General Instructions, page 174).

2. Paint pin (and stand) red with #6 flat; let dry. Add a second coat if necessary.

3. Using #2 flat throughout, paint face flesh; let dry. Using stylus, dot on black eyes. Highlight eyes with white; let dry. Blush cheeks with nearly dry brush holding just a little burgundy. Using liner, draw burgundy nose.

4. Paint hat, cloak and doll pin stand with red. Carry color into hair and fur areas slightly. Let dry.

5. Paint fur, hair and beard with white, pulling beard and fur out over cloak. Let dry.

6. Apply heavy coat of antiquing glaze to doll pin (and stand). Use soft cloth to wipe off excess, leaving glaze heavier around hair and beard to add shading. Let dry.

7. Apply a coat of satin varnish; let dry.

8. Stand doll in stand, or tie hanging loop of fine cord around top knob of clothespin. ✂

Clothespin Santa

Angelic Bathroom Accents

Dress up your guest bath with this toothbrush holder and switch plate to complete your holiday decor.

Designs by Mary Cosgrove

Materials

- Acrylic single switch plate*
- Acrylic toothbrush caddy*
- Holiday angels rub-on transfers*
- Glossy-finish interior spray varnish*
- Uncoated white paper

Fond Memories switch plate and toothbrush caddy from Crafter's Pride; Holiday Angels #CS092C Rub-On Art Color Scenes from Chartpak; Ceramcoat Interior Spray Varnish from Delta.

Instructions

1. Clean and dry surfaces of caddy and switch plate.

2. Referring to manufacturer's instructions, apply flying angels and stars rubons to switch plate, and standing angels and stars to sides of toothbrush caddy.

3. Using foam from switch plate as a pattern, cut a matching piece of white paper. Insert paper in switch plate, then foam; screw switch plate in place.

4. Using vinyl even-weave from toothbrush caddy as a pattern, cut a matching piece of white paper. Insert paper in caddy; reserve even-weave for another use. ✂

Frosty Snowman Slate

*A leftover slate round becomes a beautiful addition
to your winter decorations when you add a painted snowman.*

Design by Stan Ferraro for Delta Technical Coatings

Materials

- 10" round slate
- Acrylic paints*: black, bungalow blue, coastline blue, dark Victorian teal, light Victorian teal, pumpkin, spice brown, Tuscan red, white
- Clear glaze*
- Paintbrushes: #4 and ¾" flats, ⅛" and ⅜" deerfoots, #0 liner
- Snowflake stencil*
- Sponge
- Sealer*
- Exterior/interior matte varnish*
- Sparkling snow paint*
- Transfer paper

*Ceramcoat paints, Clear Glaze, Stencil Magic snowflake stencil #95-638-0012, All-Purpose Sealer, Exterior/Interior Matte Varnish and Sparkle Snow, all from Delta.

Background

1. Using ¾" flat brush, apply sealer to all surfaces of slate; let dry completely.

2. Apply two coats white to front and sides; let dry.

3. Enlarge pattern (page 164) 125 percent. Transfer pattern to plaque (refer to instructions for "Using Transfer and Graphite Paper" in the General Instructions, page 174).

4. *Background:* Apply clear glaze around edge of slate about 2". Do not wash out brush, but side-load with bungalow blue and go around edge, softly blending toward center in a band about 1" wide. Let dry.

5. *Snowflakes:* Mix clear glaze with equal amount coastline blue, or to make a light, transparent mixture. Choose three or four snowflakes from stencil and, using sponge, stencil seven to nine snowflakes randomly over surface. Let dry.

Painted Design

1. Work a little glaze into ⅜" deerfoot, then load toe of brush with bungalow blue and heel with coastline blue. Tap on palette to blend, then apply to snowman's lower section. Start at edges with dark color and work toward center; snowman will be fairly dark. Reload brush as needed with coastline blue. Repeat for face and ball on hat. Be sure to paint area between vest fronts.

2. Load deerfoot again, loading toe with coastline blue and heel with white. Go over all the darker blue; belly should be much lighter than edges. Tap brush and load with white frequently. Repeat for face and tip of hat.

3. Repeat step 2 using white in toe of brush and clear glaze in heel. Build up white slowly, keeping edges well blended. The deerfoot brush will make snowman "fluffy."

4. *Jacket:* Load ⅜" deerfoot with light teal on toe and white on heel. Tap in vest, keeping darker colors to outside. Wipe out brush; load toe with dark teal and heel with glaze; tap on palette to blend, then shade vest edges and under scarf.

5. *Hat:* Load ⅛" deerfoot with light teal on toe and dark teal on heel. Tap in top part of hat, then headband. Highlight, loading toe with white and heel with light teal, keeping a little clear glaze in brush.

6. *Scarf:* Load deerfoot with red in toe and pumpkin in heel. Tap in rows around neck. Shade with glaze and brown. Do tails next and finally the knot. Let dry, then tap in a few pumpkin highlights.

7. *Face:* Using ⅛" deerfoot, tap in dark areas around eyes and mouth with combined coastline blue and glaze. Paint cheeks with combined red and glaze. Load red in toe and glaze in heel. Tap in eyes with liner loaded with black; repeat for mouth.

8. *Rabbits:* Using #4 flat, base-coat with brown (see directions for base-coating in "Painting Techniques" in the General Instructions, page 174). Shade with a mixture of brown and a little black. Highlight with mixture of brown and a little white. Use small deerfoot to tap in tail, loading toe with white and heel with brown; blend on palette and tap in. Add black eyes and nose with liner.

9. *Branches and arms:* Thin brown with a little water; add branches and arms with liner. Shade with black. Paint evergreen needles with liner and thinned dark teal; add a few light teal needles to each group. Add a little sparkle snow to a few of the branches, snowman's arms and top of his hat.

10. Load ⅛" deerfoot stippler with light teal on toe and dark teal on heel. Tap in head and body of bird. Highlight with mixture of light teal and white; shade with mixture of dark teal and brown. Add eyes to beak using liner and black. ✂

Frosty Snowman Slate
Enlarge 125% before transferring

More Scrap Fabric Fun

• Make simple bows or one-knot strips for craft accents.

• Cut circles of fabric with pinking shears for jar lid covers.

• Make the latest fashion clothing and accessories for dolls.

• Make scrap Christmas ornaments.

• Cut squares or rectangles with pinking shears and make fabric wreaths covering straw wreaths.

• Cut a strip of fabric, gather and secure it to make a ruffled accent for baskets.

• Make a bandanna for your dog or cat (and one for the bird, if it insists).

• Craft some sweet-smelling sachets.

• Weave a colorful pot holder or trivet.

• Sew up some hair bows or scrunchies.

• Make treasure bags or coin purses for the kids.

Snowmen in the Moonlight

Decorative snow paste adds texture to this delightful scene
of snowmen cavorting while everyone else is asleep!

Design by Janice Higdon for Delta Technical Coatings

Left Star
Reverse for right star

Plaque

Materials

- Acrylic paints*: black, blue storm, bungalow blue, cadet, coastline blue, deep lilac, metallic silver, white
- Sparkle glaze*
- Paintbrushes: ½" and ¾", 10/0 script liner, ¼" deerfoot stippler, ¼" eagle wing
- Wooden plaque with two stars and moon*
- Sealer*
- Satin interior spray varnish*
- Snow paste*
- Palette knife
- Transfer paper
- Fine sandpaper
- Tack cloth

Ceramcoat paints and Sparkle Glaze from Delta; plaque from Provo Craft; All-Purpose Sealer, Satin Interior Spray Varnish and Decorative Tub O'Snow, all from Delta.

Plaque

1. Sand frame lightly; wipe with tack cloth. Coat with sealer; let dry.

2. Base-coat with blue storm using ¾" wash brush (refer to directions for base-coating in "Painting Techniques" in the General Instructions, page 174).

3. Paint plaque in three broad, horizontal bands, painting top third coastline blue, middle third bungalow blue and bottom third blue storm, and blend into each other while still wet. Let dry.

4. Transfer main pattern to plaque (refer to instructions for "Using Transfer and Graphite Paper" in the General Instructions, page 174).

5. *Clouds:* Wash with coastline blue; highlight with white using ½" brush.

6. *Moon:* Wash with white; float deep lilac, then white around edge fading to center. Float white back-to-back away from edge of moon. Stipple center with white using deerfoot.

7. *Snowmen:* Slip-slap bodies with coastline blue; let dry. Tap in thinned deep lilac; let dry. Stipple with white, then float around edges of body fading to center. Shade with cadet. Paint eyes and mouths black; paint noses blue storm with a little white.

8. *Rope and hula hoop:* Paint black; highlight with silver.

9. *Snow:* Slip-slap with coastline blue and bungalow blue; add a little deep lilac. Stipple with white, then float white along horizon, fading down. Shade footprints with black. Wash snow with white. Float shade of cadet around snowmen. Let dry.

10. Spray with several coats varnish, following manufacturer's instructions.

11. Following manufacturer's instructions, use palette knife to apply snow paste ¼" around scene, around edges and on back of plaque.

Moon & Stars

1. Base-coat stars with blue storm; let dry. Dry-brush coastline blue around edges with eagle wing (refer to directions for dry-brushing in "Painting Techniques" in the General Instructions, page 174).

2. Transfer star pattern to left star; reverse pattern and transfer to right star.

3. Paint snowmen as for plaque; let dry.

4. *Center star shapes:* Paint black; float with bungalow blue, using shady strokes and fading away from stars. Outline with coastline blue; let dry.

5. Spray with several coats varnish, following manufacturer's instructions.

6. Using palette knife, spread snow along edges and backs of stars and over entire moon shape; let dry.

Finishing

Apply sparkle glaze to all textured snow areas. ✄

Scrap-Happy Ornament

By Maria Nerius

You'll need a clear glass ornament for this simple project; they're readily available at most craft and art stores during the winter season. Carefully remove the ornament's cap.

Now, get out all your lightweight scraps—fabric, lace, metallic threads, feathers, small buttons, tiny beads, etc.—and cut them into smaller scraps, small enough to fit inside the ornament. Insert the desired items and replace the cap, securing it with a dab of glue.

This ornament is really dazzling on the tree, as the light reflects all the different "ingredients" inside! ✄

Ballerina Bear

Know a little girl? Chances are you know a little dancer!
A snippet of tin makes an ornament she'll cherish.
Change her skirt to a leotard for a little gymnast!

Design by Sandra Graham Smith

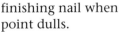

Materials

- 5" x 6" piece aluminum flashing*
- Tin snips
- Pressed-wood board
- Black fine-point permanent marker
- Glossy enamel paints: white, brown, red
- Small paintbrush
- Tracing paper
- Masking tape
- Finishing nails
- Larger nail
- Hammer
- 12" black embroidery floss
- ⅛"-wide pink satin ribbon
- 1" white eyelet lace
- Tacky craft glue

Widely available at hardware stores.

Instructions

1. Trace pattern onto tracing paper; cut out. Trace outline onto aluminum. Cut out with tin snips.

2. Tape paper pattern to aluminum. Place on pressed-wood board. Punch design using finishing nails and hammer, spacing holes evenly and replacing finishing nail when point dulls.

3. Using larger nail, punch hole in top for hanger.

4. Remove pattern and tape. Turn aluminum shape over; smooth side is back.

5. Apply paint inside punched lines using thick strokes: *muzzle—* white; *inner ears, paws and shoes—*pink (made by combining red and white); *remainder of bear—* brown. Let dry.

6. Paint laces pink; dot on eyes with white; let dry.

7. Add pupils, nose and mouth with black marker.

8. Tie ribbon in bow; glue at neck. Apply glue to bound edge of eyelet and glue in place for tutu. Thread floss through larger hole for hanger. ✂

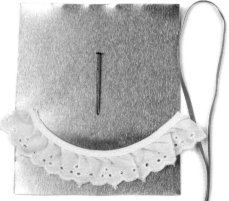

Ballerina Bear Ornament

Mosaic Candle Bowl

Translucent "grout" and scraps of glass give this candle holder a lovely glow!

Design by Debba Haupert

Materials

- Translucent soft polymer clay*
- 4"–5" glass candle bowl
- Odds and ends of sea glass or recycled glass
- "Pasta maker" for polymer clay or acrylic rod to roll out clay
- Craft knife
- Glass cleaner
- Oven

Fimo Soft polymer clay from Amaco.

Instructions

1. Clean candle bowl with glass cleaner; let dry.

2. Condition polymer clay according to manufacturer's instructions; roll out ¼" thick (setting 1 if using pasta maker).

3. Turn candle bowl upside down, then drape clay sheet over bowl, smoothing seams where clay overlaps. Using craft knife, remove clay from base of bowl. Work out any bubbles between clay and glass with your fingers.

4. Rocking glass gently to help it adhere to clay, firmly press sea glass into clay. Press bits of extra clay around and slightly over edges of glass to hold it in place securely. Continue, adding glass around sides of bowl to cover it in mosaic fashion. Hold piece up to light occasionally to make sure clay covers bowl evenly.

5. Smooth "grout" with fingers.

6. Bake as directed by polymer clay manufacturer; let cool completely. ✂

Beaded Candle Snuffer

*With a graceful wire base and engaging glass beads,
this snuffer can take on the most extravagant of candles!*

Design by Debba Haupert

Materials

- 1⅓ yards ⅛" armature wire*
- Glass drops/"marbles"
- 1⅓ yards 24-gauge tinned copper (silver) wire*
- Assorted light blue glass beads
- 1½" tapered cork
- Flat-nose pliers (optional)

WireForm WireRod armature wire from Amaco; 24-gauge wire from Artistic Wire.

Project Note

Armature wire can be easily bent with the hands. However, you may prefer to use flat-nose pliers to tighten the first curl of wire.

Instructions

1. Twist one end of armature wire in tight circle ½" across (twist around dowel or pen, if desired). Gently twist a second ring slightly larger below it to hold glass drop. Place small end of cork under glass drop and use cork as a form around which to wrap the "bell" of the snuffer, wrapping wire about six times.

2. Twist remaining wire in back-and-forth design until handle extends about 9" from base of snuffer. Twist end in spiral at end of handle; cut off excess wire.

3. Thread glass beads onto 1⅓ yards 24-gauge wire; bend wire around a bead at end to hold beads on wire.

4. At snuffer end, slide end of wire with bead under first circle of armature wire (on top of glass drop). Twist thin wire around snuffer, positioning beads randomly.

5. Spiral wire a few times around snuffer, then twist beaded wire up handle, wrapping wire at intervals

around a glass drop and securing it to handle. (Make sure glass drops face up.) Continue wrapping beaded wire around glass drops and handle of snuffer to end.

6. Twist end of 24-gauge wire around bead; secure to snuffer handle. ✀

Glittering Candle Plates

Use a few glass "marbles" to transform a plain, inexpensive glass candle saucer into a dazzling gift!

Design by Liane C. Breault

Materials

- Glass cleaner
- Glass candle plate, preferably with rimmed edge ½" wide or wider
- Flat glass marbles in desired color(s)
- Craft cement*
- Craft stick or toothpick

E6000 craft glue from Eclectic.

Instructions

1. Clean candle plate with glass cleaner; let dry completely.

2. Without applying glue, arrange marbles around rim of candle saucer as desired.

3. One by one, carefully apply glue to back of each marble with craft stick or toothpick and position on rim of candle plate.

4. Let dry at least 24 hours. ✂

Wire-Wrapped Candle Cubes

Dress up simple cube candles with wires and beads for glittering gifts!

Designs by Katie Hacker

Materials
Each Candle
- ½ cup white candle wax*
- Candle dye and fragrance*
- 2½" clear glass votive cube
- 5" wick and clip*
- 24" 20-gauge wire*
- 6mm glass bead
- Pliers
- Craft stick
- Dowel or pencil
- Double boiler
- Candy thermometer
- Stove
- Old newspaper

Yaley Enterprises wax, dye, fragrance, wick and clip; Beadalon Colourcraft wire.

Candle

1. String wick through clip; crimp with pliers. Break wax into 1"–2" pieces; melt in top of double boiler following manufacturer's instructions, stirring frequently with craft stick and monitoring temperature with candy thermometer. Add small shavings of dye until desired color is reached.

2. Dip wick clip in melted wax; press in bottom of votive with craft stick. Lay dowel or pencil across top of votive; wrap wick around it to hold wick straight; secure with tape.

3. Pour wax into votive, then let candle cool without moving. When cool, trim wick to ¼".

Wire Decoration

1. Wrap wire around top of votive, bringing ends to front and twisting twice.

2. Form wire ends in pattern of coils, spirals, loops and/or figure-eights as desired, securing bead on one end of wire. ✀

From the Heart

Many of us scrap crafters create items that we will donate to a good cause. There are also dozens of national programs that prize handmade blankets, greeting cards, quilts, afghans, hats, baby clothes and toys made from scraps. There is no greater gift than a craft made from the heart. Here are some things to consider as you scrap crafts for charity.

- Check with the charity, hospital or other intended recipient for any guidelines or requirements they may have.

- All fabrics should be machine washable and dryable. Cotton, polyester and cotton/poly blends are good fabric choices. All fabrics should be prewashed to eliminate shrinkage.

- Acrylic yarns are a better choice than cotton yarns because cotton yarn may shrink. Finish yarn and thread ends securely.

- Items intended for babies or toddlers should be made of soft materials. The seams and finishes should also be gentle on a child's skin.

- Make sure the item is securely constructed.

- Zigzag, serge, use pinking shears or otherwise finish exposed cut edges of woven fabrics to prevent fraying. Knit fabrics usually do not fray. Cut edges that are completely enclosed (such as those inside a collar or a quilt) are not subject to the abrasion that causes fraying.

- Launder finished items as you might expect the recipient to launder it before giving them away. If you launder the finished item, any change in appearance will take place and the recipient won't feel they have harmed the item when they launder it. Laundering also helps remove pet hair, cigarette smoke and other contaminants that might cause an allergic reaction.

- Use yarn or heavy thread—not pins or safety pins—to attach sets together.

- Provide a care tag with laundering instructions. Use yarn or thread to attach the tag and leave a large enough loop that it can be easily cut to remove the tag without damaging the attached item.

- A Web site called Sewing Charity offers an extensive list of charities and organizations that can always use some heartfelt and handmade items: www.dotdigital.com/sewing charity/recipients.html

General Instructions

Materials

In addition to the materials listed for each craft, some of the following supplies may be needed to complete your projects.

General Crafts

- Paper Towels
- Scissors
- Pencil
- Ruler
- Tracing paper
- Craft knife
- Heavy-duty craft cutters or wire nippers
- Masking tape
- Plenty of newspapers to protect work surface
- Safety goggles

Painted Items

- Paper towels
- Paper or plastic foam plate or tray for holding and mixing paints
- Plastic—a garbage bag, grocery sack, etc.—to protect work surface
- Container of water or other fluid for cleaning brushes

Fabric Projects

- Iron and ironing board
- Pressing cloth
- Basic sewing notions
- Rotary cutter and self-healing mat
- Air-soluble markers
- Tailor's chalk

Reproducing Patterns & Templates

The patterns provided in this book are shown right side up, as they should look on the finished project; a few oversize patterns that need to be enlarged are clearly marked. Photocopiers with enlarging capabilities are readily available at copy stores and office supply stores. Copy the page, setting the photocopier to enlarge the pattern to the percentage indicated.

Patterns that do not need to be enlarged may be reproduced by placing a piece of tracing paper or vellum over the pattern in the book, and tracing the outlines carefully with a pencil or other marker.

Once you've copied your pattern pieces, cut them out and use these pieces as templates to trace around. Secure them as needed with pins or pattern weights.

If you plan to reuse the patterns or if the patterns are more intricate, with sharp points, etc., make sturdier templates by gluing the copied page of patterns onto heavy cardboard or template plastic. Let the glue dry, then cut out the pieces with a craft knife.

Depending on the application, it may be preferable to trace the patterns onto the wrong side of the fabric or other material so that no lines will be visible from the front. In this case, make sure you place the right side of the pattern piece against the wrong side of the fabric, paper or other material so that the piece will face the right direction when it is cut out.

Using Transfer & Graphite Paper

Read the manufacturer's instructions for using transfer or graphite paper before beginning.

Lay tracing paper over printed pattern and trace; then place transfer paper transfer side down on material to be marked. Lay traced pattern on top. Secure layers with low-tack masking tape or tacks to keep pattern and transfer paper from shifting. Then using a stylus or pen, retrace pattern lines using smooth, even pressure.

Painted Designs

Disposable paper and plastic foam plates make good palettes for pouring and mixing paints.

Follow instructions carefully with regard to initial preparations—sanding, applying primer and/or a base coat of color. Take special care when painting adjacent sections with different colors; allow the first color to dry so that the second will not run or mix. When adding designs atop a painted base, let the base coat dry thoroughly first.

If you will be mixing media, such as drawing with marking pens on a painted surface, test the process and your materials on scraps to make sure there will be no running or bleeding.

Keep your work surface and tools clean. Clean brushes promptly in the manner recommended by the paint manufacturer; many acrylics can be cleaned up with soap and water, while other paints may require a solvent. Suspend paintbrushes by their handles to dry so that the fluid drains out completely and bristles remain straight and undamaged.

Work in a well-ventilated area; read product labels thoroughly to be aware of any potential hazards and precautions.

Painting Techniques

Base-coating: Load paintbrush evenly with color by dabbing it on palette, then coat surfaces with one or two smooth, solid coats of paint, letting paint dry between coats.

Dry-brushing: Dip a dry round-bristle brush in paint; wipe excess paint off onto paper towel until brush is almost dry. Wipe brush across edges for subtle shading.

Rouging: Dip dry round-bristle brush in paint; wipe off onto paper towel until brush is almost completely dry and leaves no visible brush strokes. Wipe brush across area to be rouged using a circular motion.

Shading: Dip brush in water and blot lightly once on paper towel, leaving some water in brush. Dip point of brush into paint. Stroke onto palette once or twice to blend paint into water on bristles so that stroke has paint on one side gradually blending to no color on the other side. Apply to project as directed. ✄

Designer Index

Technique Index

Buyer's Guide

Projects in this book were made using products provided by the manufacturers listed below. Look for the suggested products in your local craft- and art-supply stores. If unavailable, contact suppliers below. Some may be able to sell products directly to you; others may be able to refer you to retail sources.

Aldastar Pom Beadz
Available through:
Craft Supplies by ArtCove
www.artcove.com/
Pompoms/Pombeadz/
pombeadz.shtml

Aleene's/div. of Duncan Enterprises
5673 E. Shields Ave.
Fresno, CA 93727
(800) 237-2642
www.duncan-
enterprises.com

**Amaco
American Art Clay Co. Inc.**
4717 W. 16th St.
Indianapolis, IN
46222-2598
(317) 244-6871
www.amaco.com

API/Adhesive Products Inc.
520 Cleveland Ave.
Albany, CA 94710
(510) 526-7616
www.crafterspick.com

Artistic Wire Ltd.
1210 Harrison Ave.
La Grange Park, IL
60526
(630) 530-7567
www.artisticwire.com

Arty's/The Janlynn Corp.
P.O. Box 51848
Indian Orchard, MA
01151-5848
(800) 445-5565
www.artys.ch

**Beacon Adhesives/
Signature Marketing**
P.O. Box 427
Wyckoff, NJ 07481
(800) 865-7238
www.beacon1.com

Beadalon
www.beadalon.com
(800) 824-9473

The Beadery
P.O. Box 178
Hope Valley, RI 02832
(401) 539-2432

Beck Hill Group
175 Bryant Ave.

Gen Ellyn, IL 60137
(630) 858-2015
www.popuppaper.com

ChartPak Rub-On Art
1 River Rd.
Leeds, MA 01053
(800) 628-1910

**C.M. Offray & Son Inc./
Lion Ribbon Co. Inc.**
Route 24, Box 601
Chester, NJ 07930-0601
(800) 555-LION
www.offray.com

Clearsnap Inc.
Box 98
Anacortes, WA 98221
(360) 293-6634
www.clearsnap.com

Craft Catalog
P.O. Box 1069
Reynoldsbury, OH
43068
(800) 777-1442
www.craftcatalog.com

Crafter's Pick by API
520 Cleveland Ave.
Albany, CA 94710
(510) 526-7616
www.crafterspick.com

**Crafter's Pride/
Daniel Enterprises**
P.O. Box 1105
Laurinburg, NC 28353
(910) 277-7441
www.crafterspride.com

Creative Beginnings
P.O. Box 1330
Morro Bay, CA 93442
(800) 367-1739
www.creative-
beginnings.com

D&CC
428 S. Zelta
Wichita, KS 67207
(800) 835-3013
e-mail: dcc@feist.com

Darice Inc.
Mail-order source:
Bolek's
330 N. Tuscarawas Ave.
Dover, OH 44622
(330) 364-8878

DecoArt
P.O. Box 386

Stanford, KY 40484
(800) 367-3047
www.decoart.com

Delta Technical Coatings
2550 Pellissier Pl.
Whittier, CA 90601-1505
(800) 423-4135
www.deltacrafts.com

Déjà Views/The C-Thru Ruler Co.
6 Britton Dr.
Bloomfield, CT
06002-3602
(800) 243-0303
www.cthruruler.com

DMD Industries Inc./The Paper Reflections Line
1250 ESI Dr.
Springdale, AR
72764
(800) 805-9890
www.dmdind.com

**Dow Flora Craft/
Dow Chemical Co.**
(800) 441-4369

Duncan Enterprises
5673 E. Shields Ave.
Fresno, CA 93727
(800) 237-2642
www.duncancrafts.com

Eclectic Products Inc.
995 S. A St.
Springfield, OR 97477
(800) 693-4667

EK Success Ltd.
125 Entin Rd.
Clifton, NJ 07014
(800) 524-1349
www.eksuccess.com

Fibre-Craft Materials Corp.
Mail-order source:
Kirchen Brothers
P.O. Box 1016
Skokie, IL 60076
(800) 378-5024
e-mail: kirchenbro@
aol.com

Fiskars Inc.
7811 W. Stewart Ave.
Wausau, WI 54401
(800) 950-0203,
ext. 1277
www.fiskars.com

**Forster Inc./
Diamond Brands**
1800 Cloquet
Cloquet, MN 55720
(218) 879-6700
www.diamondbrands
.com/forster.html

Gourd Central
7264 St. Rte. 314
Mount Gilead, OH
43338
(419) 362-9201
www.gourdcentral.com

Halcraft USA
30 W. 24th St.
New York, NY 10010
(212) 376-1580
www.halcraft.com

Hands of the Hills
3016 78th Ave. S.E.
Mercer Island, WA
98040
(206) 232-4588
www.hohbead.com

Hearts and Crafts!
P.O. Box 2063
Meford Lakes, NJ
08055

Highsmith Corp.
P.O. Box 800
Fort Atkinson, WI
53538-0800
(800) 554-4661

Hot Off the Press Inc.
1250 N.W. Third
Canby, OR 97013
(888) 826-7255
www.craftpizazz.com

J.B. Wood Products
P.O. Box 3084
South Attleboro, MA
02703

Jones Tones Inc.
33685 United Ave.
Pueblo, CO 81001
(719) 948-0048
www.sales@
jonestones.com

**Krylon/Sherwin-
Williams Co.**
Craft Customer Service
101 Prospect Ave. N.W.
Cleveland, OH 44115
(800) 247-3268
www.krylon.com

Kunin Felt Co./Foss Mfg. Co. Inc.
P.O. Box 5000
Hampton, NH
03842-5000
(603) 929-6100
www.kuninfelt.com

Lara's Crafts
590 N. Beach St.
Fort Worth, TX 76111
(800) 232-5272
www.larascrafts.com

Milestones Products Co.
15127 N.E. 24th,
Ste. 332
Redmond, WA
98052-5547
(425) 882-1987

Paper Adventures
P.O. Box 04393
Milwaukee, WI
53204-0393
(800) 727-0699
www.paperadventures
.com

**Paper Reflections/
DMD Industries Inc.**
23005 Old Missouri Rd.
Springdale, AR 72764
(800) 805-9890
www.dmdind.com

Pellon Consumer Products
3440 Industrial Dr.
Durham, NC 27704
(919) 620-3916

Plaid Enterprises Inc.
3225 Westech Dr.
Norcross, GA 30092
(800) 842-4197
www.plaidonline.com

Provo Craft
Mail-order source:
Creative Express
295 W. Center St.
Provo, UT 84601-4436
(800) 563-8679
www.creativeexpress.com

**Sculpey III/
Polyform Products Co.**
1901 Estes Ave.
Elk Grove Village, IL
60007
(847) 427-0020
www.sculpey.com

Therm O Web
770 Glenn Ave.
Wheeling, IL 60090
(847) 520-5200
www.thermoweb.com

Toner Plastics
699 Silver St.
Agawam, MA 01001
(413) 789-1300
www.tonerplastics.com

Tulip/div. of Duncan Enterprises
5673 E. Shields Ave.,
Fresno, CA 93727
(800) 237-2642
www.duncan-
enterprises.com

V.I.P. Fabrics
1412 Broadway
New York, NY 10018
(800) 847-4064

Walnut Hollow Farms Inc.
1409 St. Rd. 23
Dodgeville, WI
53533-2112
(800) 950-5101
www.walnuthollow.com

**Warm & Natural/
The Warm Co.**
954 E. Union St.
Seattle, WA 98122
(800) 234-WARM
www.warmcompany
.com

Wimpole Street Creations
Mail-order source:
Barrett House
P.O. Box 540585
North Salt Lake, UT
84054-0585
(801) 299-0700
e-mail: wimpole@
xmission.com

Wrights
P.O. Box 398
West Warren, MA 01092
(413) 436-7732,
ext. 445
www.wrights.com

Yaley
7664 Avianca Dr.
Redding, CA 96002
(530) 365-5252
www.yaley.com